ANOTHER TIME

In memory of my brother
RALPH HORWITZ
(1926–1988)

RONALD HARWOOD

ANOTHER TIME

AMBER LANE PRESS

All rights whatsoever in this play are strictly reserved
and application for performance, etc. must be made
before rehearsals begin to:

Judy Daish Associates Ltd.
83 Eastbourne Mews
London W2 6LQ

No performance may be given unless a licence has been
obtained.

First published in 1989 by
Amber Lane Press Ltd
Cheorl House
Church Street
Charlbury, Oxon OX7 3PR
Telephone: 0608 810024

Printed in Great Britain by
Bocardo Press Ltd., Didcot, Oxfordshire

ISBN 0 906399 98 X

CONDITIONS OF SALE

CHARACTERS

IKE LANDS:	aged 61
LEONARD LANDS:	aged 16 and 51
BELLE LANDS:	aged 49 and 84
PROFESSOR ZADOK SALT:	aged 54 and 89
ROSE SALT:	aged 51 and 86
JEREMY LANDS:	aged 18
TWO TECHNICIANS:	(Act Two)

Note: The actor who plays IKE in Act One plays LEONARD in Act Two.

The actor who plays LEONARD in Act One plays JEREMY in Act Two.

ACT ONE
(Early 1950s)

The small ground-floor flat belonging to Belle and Ike Lands in Sea Point, Cape Town.

Scene One: The hall, 6.30 p.m. on a winter evening in June.

Scene Two: Belle's bedroom, at approximately the same time on the same evening.

Scene Three: The hall, a moment later.

Scene Four: Belle's bedroom, a week later.

ACT TWO
(Thirty-five years later)

A recording studio in Maida Vale, London.

Scene One: The studio, shortly before 1 p.m.

Scene Two: The control booth, at approximately the same time on the same day.

Scene Three: The studio.

Scene Four: The control booth.

Another Time was first presented by Duncan C. Weldon and Jerome Minskoff for Triumph Theatre Productions Ltd. at the Theatre Royal, Bath, on 22nd August 1989, and subsequently at Wyndham's Theatre, London, on 25th September 1989 with the following cast:

ACT ONE
(Early 1950s)

IKE LANDS:	Albert Finney
LEONARD LANDS:	Christien Anholt
BELLE LANDS:	Janet Suzman
PROFESSOR ZADOK SALT:	David de Keyser
ROSE SALT:	Sara Kestelman

ACT TWO
(Thirty-five years later)

LEONARD LANDS:	Albert Finney
JEREMY LANDS:	Christien Anholt
BELLE LANDS:	Janet Suzman
PROFESSOR ZADOK SALT:	David de Keyser
ROSE SALT:	Sara Kestelman

Directed by Elijah Moshinsky

Designed by Saul Radomsky

Lighting by Paul Pyant

ACT ONE

Early 1950s.

The pentagonal hall of a small ground-floor flat.

The hall is used as a dining room but is also a thoroughfare. There is a front door, which leads to a path that leads to the street; a door to BELLE's *bedroom; a short passage off which there are other doors (not necessarily visible) to* IKE *and* LEONARD's *bedroom, the bathroom, living room and kitchen. There is a dining table in a polished dark wood with four matching chairs, and a modern desk-cum-bookcase.*

SCENE ONE

The hall. 6.30 p.m.

IKE LANDS, *aged 61, sits at the table reading a volume of an encyclopaedia. He is a handsome man with a lame left hand on which he wears a brown leather glove. He turns the pages with the third finger of his right hand which he first moistens on his tongue. He occasionally reacts audibly to what he reads: a tuneless whistle or clucking his teeth.*

After he has turned a page or two, his son, LEONARD LANDS, *aged 16, enters, carrying a music case and a satchel, He is dressed in school uniform: a black blazer, white shirt and tie, and grey flannels.*

IKE: Leonard!

LEONARD: Hello, Dad.

[LEONARD *is about to go into his bedroom.*]

IKE: Don't I get a kiss?

[LEONARD *kisses him on the cheek.*]

And how's Arthur Rubenstein this evening?

LEONARD: Dad, I'm not Arthur Rubenstein.

IKE: Did you have a good lesson?

LEONARD: Fine. Mom and Aunty Rose were on the bus. I came back with them. They're outside talking to Miss Anna Katz.

IKE: A very cultured woman. You going to practise now?

LEONARD: No. I've some homework to do first —

[*He goes to the desk and starts to unpack his satchel.*]

[BELLE LANDS *enters. She is 49 years old, a once beautiful woman, but now tired and anxious.*]

Where's Aunty Rose?

BELLE: Still talking to Anna Katz. I'm too tired to stand and listen.

[*She crosses to her bedroom door.*]

Leonard, ask your father if he's in for supper.

LEONARD: [*as a matter of course*] Dad, Mom wants to know if you're in for supper.

IKE: Tell her of course I'm in for supper, when am I out?

LEONARD: Yes, he's in for supper.

BELLE: I'm going to make a cup of tea for Rose and me. Ask your father if he wants tea or coffee.

LEONARD: Dad, do you want tea or coffee?

IKE: [*a shrug*] Anything.

[*BELLE goes into the kitchen.*]

Leonard, before you start on your homework, will you do me a favour?

LEONARD: What?

IKE: Don't say what like that. I'm not going to ask you to climb Table Mountain.

LEONARD: I'm sorry, what's the favour?

IKE: Will you cut my fingernails for me?

LEONARD: [*after a slight hesitation*] Yes, of course.

[IKE *removes his glove from his lame hand.* LEONARD *finds a pair of nail scissors, sits by his father and starts to cut his fingernails.*]

IKE: People think I should be able to cut the nails of my bad hand myself. But I can't. I don't know why. I can't.

[ROSE SALT *enters. She is 51, a spinster, energetic and intelligent.* LEONARD *continues to cut his father's nails.*]

ROSE: Good evening, Ike —

IKE: Hello, Rose, how goes it?

ROSE: I'm fine. Is Belle in her room?

LEONARD: No, she's making tea.

IKE: So, Rose, I've been meaning to ask you, what do you hear about this new book?

ROSE: What new book?

IKE: This American *Naked and the Dead* business by this fellow, what's-his-name?

ROSE: Mailer, Norman Mailer. Ike, it's filth. Have nothing to do with it. Don't have it in the house.

[BELLE *returns with a tray with a pot of tea, two cups and a glass of water. She puts the glass of water in front of* IKE.]

IKE: Ask your mother what's this.

LEONARD: What's this, Mom?

BELLE: I asked him if he wants tea or coffee and he said anything, so I brought him a glass of water.

ROSE: [*laughing*] Belle, you're a cow —

IKE: [*under his breath*] God Almighty —

BELLE: [*also laughing*] Well, he said anything —

IKE: [*louder; dangerous*] God Almighty —

BELLE: Tell him to keep his shirt on. Get a cup from the kitchen —

ROSE: I'll go —

[*She exits into the kitchen.*]

BELLE: [*to* LEONARD] Leonard, you need a haircut.

LEONARD: Mom, I have to talk to you —

BELLE: So, come and talk.

LEONARD: I want to look at some maths first.

[ROSE *returns with a cup and saucer. She pours* IKE *a cup of tea.*]

BELLE: Leonard, why don't you work in the lounge or the bedroom, what d'you want to work in here for?

LEONARD: I prefer it here —

BELLE: You prefer it here, it's like a railway station and you prefer it here. I don't know how you can concentrate —

ROSE: Milk and sugar, Ike?

IKE: Sugar, no milk, thank you.

[BELLE *goes to her bedroom door and opens it.* ROSE *gives* IKE *his tea and then follows her.*]

BELLE: I'll be in my room —

LEONARD: I won't be a moment —

ROSE: Belle, you'll never guess what Ike just asked me —

BELLE: That's true —

[*They go, closing the door.*]

IKE: What did I just ask her? I asked her about a book. What's the fuss? Do they think I don't know what goes on in this world?

[LEONARD *continues to cut* IKE's *nails.* IKE *sips his tea.*]

LEONARD: Dad, if you don't keep still I'll cut you.

IKE: Worse things can happen.

[LEONARD *cuts.* IKE *reads. From* BELLE's *room, laughter.*]
Thick as thieves, those two sisters, thick as thieves. The whole Salt family was very close-knit. Like an island. Very independent. Well, look at your mother and Rose. Your Uncle Zadok's the best of the bunch. Their father, old Leopold Salt, Leonard, was a Freethinker. Enough

said. Your other grandfather, my father, was a wonderful whistler. I often think that's where you get your musical talent. Don't tell your mother.

[*He reads.* LEONARD *cuts.*]

The stuff they put in these books. Listen to this, d'you know what procaine hydrochloride is?

LEONARD: No.

IKE: An anaesthetic introduced in 1905 under the trade name Novocaine.

[BELLE*'s door opens a crack. Neither* IKE *nor* LEONARD *notice.*]

Things like that are interesting. You should read these, Sir John Hammerton's Book of Knowledge, Leonard, I bought them for you —

BELLE: *I* bought them for him.

[IKE *and* LEONARD *look round and* BELLE *closes the door. Silence.*]

IKE: What a bad hand I was dealt.

LEONARD: You mean this hand, your paralysed hand?

IKE: No, I mean a hand of cards, the shuffle of life, the deal, the deal, the cards you get, the hand you're given to play in the game of life. You, you've been dealt a Royal Flush, thank God, unbeatable, a great musical talent, you play the piano like Franz Liszt and you're not seventeen yet, a genius, what a hand you've got, but me, I got a hand with fours high. You know why I say this? Because I think by nature I could have been a scholar. I love books, Leonard, like your mother and your Aunty Rose. I love learning. But what chance did I have? What chance did any of my generation have? We were refugees, immigrants, if we had talents or gifts or inclinations no one knew, no one cared. We had only one obligation. To make a living. To survive. We were never allowed to be what we really were. That's an accident of history, a rotten shuffle, a hand fours high. No, no, no. I love learning.

[*Silence.*]

[*lowering his voice*] Leonard, are you smoking cigarettes?

LEONARD: No, Dad —

IKE: Tell me the truth, Leonard —

LEONARD: No, Dad —

IKE: I'm not going to get cross —

LEONARD: I'm not smoking, Dad —

IKE: I'm desperate for a cigarette, Len. [*Pause.*] I just want one of your cigarettes.

> [*Pause.* LEONARD *takes a packet of ten cigarettes from his music case and gives* IKE *one.*]

IKE: [*noting the packet*] Sir Seymour, eh?

LEONARD: [*an urgent whisper*] Don't tell Mummy.

> [IKE *lights up and puffs deeply.*]

IKE: I wonder how much they paid him.

LEONARD: Who?

IKE: Sir Seymour, Sir Seymour Hicks.

LEONARD: You should know, you sold the cigarettes —

IKE: They never told me. People like me don't get told things like that. That kind of information is all Head Office. They never tell the commercial travellers anything. And anyway, it was never a good line. People like the old brands. New brands are difficult. But they must have paid him something. I mean, a famous actor gives his name to cigarettes, he's got to be paid a few bob. [*looks at the packet*] Can't be a bad deal. You give your name, they put your photograph on the packet and he's not even in Sir John Hammerton's Book of Knowledge. He was dealt a good hand, that's all, and he never looked much of an actor to me. Now, Ronald Colman, that's a different story. Perhaps they would have liked to have named a cigarette after Ronald Colman, but there's already the mustard, so you're in trouble. Still, I bet Sir Seymour was well paid. And du Maurier. And that singer fellow, De Reszke. One day, please God, you'll have a cigarette named after you. No, no, Leonard, plastic hangers is the coming thing. I'm telling you, there's a fortune in plastic hangers. If I could just bring off this one deal, get the agency for these plastic hangers, we'd never have to worry again. [*puffs deeply*] I was dying for a cigarette. [*Pause.*] Len, you haven't got a couple of bob on you, have you?

LEONARD: No, I spent all I had on the cigarettes, I'm sorry. [*Pause.*] Dad —

IKE: What?

LEONARD: I've got something to tell you.

IKE: Bad news?

LEONARD: I had my lesson with Professor Kinski this afternoon —

IKE: And?

LEONARD: He thinks I ought to go overseas to study. To Vienna.
          [*Silence.*]
          You think there's any chance?
          [*Silence.*]
     IKE: [*a sigh*] Money, money, money, money.
LEONARD: Yes, I know, never mind, Dad —
     IKE: Len, it's like I always say, it's not what you know,
          it's who you know —
          [*Silence.*]
LEONARD: I better talk to Mummy about Vienna.
          [*Silence.*]
     IKE: You know where I'd like to go?
LEONARD: Where?
     IKE: Pompeii. Pompeii and Herculaneum. I was reading
          about them this afternoon. According to Sir John
          Hammerton you can see the ruins of both cities on the
          same day. What a trip that would be, eh? Destroyed by
          a volcano. Just imagine it, Len, you're sitting there
          having your breakfast or reading a book or practising
          the piano, and suddenly no warning, whooosh! Gone.
          And it's all preserved for you to see. That's history for
          you. That's being in the wrong place at the wrong time.
          I sometimes feel —
          [*Silence.*]
LEONARD: I must do my homework.
          [*He goes to the desk and starts to unpack his satchel.*]
   BELLE: [*off*] Leonard, come and talk to us, your maths
          can wait —
          [LEONARD *rises. As he crosses to* BELLE's *door the front
          doorbell rings.*]
LEONARD: [*putting his head into* BELLE's *room*] There's someone at the
          door —
   BELLE: [*off*] It'll be Uncle Zadok, your father can let him in.
          [LEONARD *hesitates for a moment but goes to the front door
          and opens it to* PROFESSOR ZADOK SALT, *aged 54.*]
   ZADOK: Maestro!
          [*He squeezes* LEONARD's *cheeks with grunts of pleasure.*
          LEONARD *hates this.*]
          Ike, good evening.
     IKE: Hello, Zadok, I'm pleased to see you. Your sisters are
          in there.
   ZADOK: But it's you I've come to visit.
     IKE: Me?
   BELLE: [*off*] Leonard, is Uncle Zadok there?

LEONARD: [*calling*] Yes, he's here —

ZADOK: I'm not staying long —

[*He crosses to* BELLE'*s door, knocks and opens it.*]

Sisters mine, it's your brudder.

BELLE: [*off*] Hello, Zadok —

ROSE: [*off*] Hello, Zadok —

BELLE: [*off*] Tell Leonard to come and see me —

ZADOK: [*shutting the door*] Maestro, your mother wants to see you —

LEONARD: Coming, Mom —

ZADOK: Ike, I'm starving —

IKE: So, go into the kitchen, open the fridge and find something. It's the maid's night off.

[ZADOK *goes into the kitchen.*]

[LEONARD *considers for a moment, then goes to his music case, takes out the packet of cigarettes and slips two of them to* IKE. IKE *shudders, controlling tears.*]

LEONARD: For God's sake, don't cry, Dad —

IKE: [*crying*] You've got such a good heart — I'm sorry — I'm sorry — God Almighty, what a life — [*recovering*] Go and see your mother. Don't put her in a worse mood than she's in already.

[LEONARD *goes into* BELLE'*s room as* ZADOK *returns, eating a chicken leg. He puts his head into* BELLE'*s bedroom.*]

ZADOK: I've stolen a chicken leg.

[*He closes the door.*]

So, Ike, how are you?

IKE: So-so. I get these pains in my stomach.

ZADOK: Take a laxative.

IKE: I take but nothing happens. So, what d'you want to see me about?

ZADOK: I want to talk to you.

IKE: It's not my birthday, you know.

[ZADOK *sits.*]

ZADOK: Ike, how's the hand?

IKE: It gets cold in this weather.

ZADOK: And the leg?

IKE: The same.

ZADOK: Listen, Ike, just listen to what I've got to say. As you well know, I'm a dry, dusty, unemotional man, so I'm going to put this in a dry, dusty and unemotional way.

IKE: I'm listening —

ZADOK: I happened to meet David Figg the other day, he's the best G.P. in town, the top man, and we had a chat about you. He said to me, 'With Ike Lands, it's mind over matter.'

IKE: What's mind over matter?

ZADOK: Your hand.

IKE: My hand's mind over matter?

ZADOK: According to Dr. Figg, if you wanted to use it, you'd use it.

IKE: [*showing him the gloved hand*] I want to use it, Zadok.

ZADOK: I'm only quoting Dr. David Figg. What's your own doctor say?

IKE: Simons? Nathan Simons, round the corner? What does Dr. Simons say about my hand? He says, 'I've never seen a hand like this', that's what he says. That man Simons, I'd like to see his certificate, I don't think he ever qualified. Simons, what does he know? He knows 'take two aspirin' and 'come and see me when your temperature's down.' Simons, I'd be better off with a vet.

ZADOK: David Figg says your hand is mind over matter. And he says the same is probably true of your bad leg. Consider the facts, Ike. Your mother dies, you have a — a crisis —

IKE: It was a breakdown, call a spade a spade. I'm not ashamed, it was a nervous breakdown. I grieved until my heart broke —

[*He shudders with tears.*]

ZADOK: Now that was before the war —

IKE: 1935, just after Leonard was born, 7 January 1935, that's the anniversary of her death, fifteen years ago, God rest her soul. They were difficult times. But then the war came and I liked it in the army —

ZADOK: Ike, I never understood how you got into the army. What did the army doctor say when you showed him your hand?

IKE: I didn't show it to him. He didn't ask so I didn't show. Army doctors, doctors. [*waves them away*] No, but I liked the army. The pay was regular. They sent Belle some money each month. Back pay, they called it. She was happy then. Happier. And then, with my luck, I'm demobbed a year and I have to go and get knocked down by a car.

ZADOK: And your leg goes lame. Now, what David Figg is saying is that there may be a psychological cause. You get these terrible shocks, your mother's death, the accident, and they manifest themselves physically. That's what he means by mind over matter.

IKE: Is that what you came specially to tell me, mind over matter?

ZADOK: Look, Ike, we've been friends since before you became my brother-in-law. David Figg says the best man to have a look at you is Norman Hurwitz, this man is the top psychiatrist in the country, he's a professor —

IKE: A psychiatrist —?

ZADOK: A professor of psychiatry —

IKE: You think I should see a psychiatrist?

ZADOK: Why not? It's not shameful, a paralysed hand isn't the plague, it's not catching, it's not syphilis —

IKE: Please, Zadok —

ZADOK: Go and see him, what can you lose?

IKE: [*after a moment*] What can I lose? Only a paralysed hand, I suppose.

ZADOK: And a gammy leg.

IKE: Is that what you wanted to see me about?

ZADOK: Should I arrange an appointment with Professor Hurwitz?

IKE: You know him?

ZADOK: Certainly.

IKE: You know everybody, eh, Zadok?

ZADOK: As you've always said, Ike, 'It's not what you know —'

IKE: [*joining in*] — 'It's who you know.'
    [*They laugh quietly.*]
    I'm glad you came tonight, Zadok.

ZADOK: Ike, it's always a pleasure to see you.

IKE: You've got a moment?

ZADOK: A moment.

IKE: You can't stay for supper?

ZADOK: No, I've got to give a lecture tomorrow, I have to prepare —

IKE: I don't see a lot of people these days. So, tell me, you like being a professor?

ZADOK: Too much administration, not enough teaching. I'm a better teacher than administrator but, yes, I like it.

IKE: Such a wonderful title.

ZADOK: What?

IKE: Professor of Moral Philosophy.

ZADOK: I'm glad you're impressed.

IKE: I'd have given anything to be a Professor of Moral

Philosophy. Tell you what, I'd have given anything just to have gone to a university. I'm not cut out for commerce, Zadok. Tell you the truth, I would never say this to Belle, I'm not a businessman —

ZADOK: Things will turn the corner, Ike —

IKE: Yes, turn the corner, I'll turn the corner and what'll I find? Another cul-de-sac. Like the fish shop. What bad luck we had there. Everybody before and since has made a fortune out of that fish shop, but not me. I don't know, somehow, I just can't seem to — to —

ZADOK: Everything's going to come out right, mark my words.

IKE: From your mouth into God's ear.

ZADOK: You've got something going?

IKE: I might get an agency for plastic hangers.

ZADOK: Sounds good.
      [*Silence.*]
      And that son of yours, that Leonard, I could eat him —

IKE: You honestly think he's the real thing, Zadok?

ZADOK: I know it. I've talked to people, people who understand music, expert people, everyone's agreed that Leonard has genius.

IKE: Genius, really?

ZADOK: People who've heard him play and, incidentally, I don't know how much he tells you, but you know Miss Anna Katz, she went to his recital and she says he plays like Rachmaninoff.

IKE: Kinski, you know his teacher, Otto Kinski, he's also a professor, Viennese, a refugee from Hitler —

ZADOK: I know him —

IKE: He thinks Leonard should go overseas to study.

ZADOK: I'm not surprised.
      [*Laughter from* BELLE's *room.*]
      [IKE *suddenly heaves with suppressed crying.*]
      Ike, what's the trouble — what's the matter — ?

IKE: I don't want to let that boy down —

ZADOK: What are you talking about, why should you let him down?

IKE: How can I afford to send him to Vienna? I can't afford a packet of cigarettes —
      [IKE *cries.* ZADOK *is horribly embarrassed.*]
      God Almighty, what a life —

ZADOK: We'll find a way, we'll all club together.
      [*Silence.*]

IKE: It's cruel, Zadok, it's cruel —

ZADOK: What is?

IKE: Life, history, it's cruel —

ZADOK: You know what, Ike? You would have made a good Professor of Moral Philosophy.

IKE: Don't I know? My head is full of knowledge and no way to use it. Did you know, for example, that procaine hydrochloride is an anaesthetic introduced in 1905 under the trade name Novocaine?

ZADOK: No, I didn't know that —

IKE: You see what I mean? Take this hand of mine — [*holds up his gloved hand*] — I understand this to be a symbol of my life, I understand things like that —

ZADOK: Don't be a bloody fool, Ike, symbols of life aren't that easy to come by —

[*The sound of* BELLE *laughing.*]

IKE: She's happy tonight. But listen to me, Zadok, I've got this useless hand, useless, I can't move it, not a finger, it's like my life, a bum hand, you can't win the game with a bum hand of cards, you can't have a life —

ZADOK: We're all dealt bum hands, Ike —

IKE: Nonsense, that's nonsense —

ZADOK: Ike, we all have our tragedies, our hardships. You think I asked for my wife to die three months after we were married?

IKE: That's different, death's entirely different, I'm talking about struggle. I've had to struggle like no one else I know — I've had such bad luck — the world's been against me, Zadok —

ZADOK: Ike, I'm going to talk to you straight, the world's not against you. 'The fault, dear Brutus —'

[LEONARD *returns, closing* BELLE*'s door, goes to the desk and takes books out of his satchel.*]

[*without interruption*] '— is not in our stars, but in ourselves', ourselves, Ike, the fault is in us, in me, in you —

IKE: I'm responsible for my bad hand?

ZADOK: Listen to me, Leonard, you listen to me, too. I've got something important to say. There is no justice in this life. Remember that. There is no justice.

[LEONARD *exits.*]

[*Silence.*]

IKE: Failure. Yes. It's a terrible thing to be a failure. That's what Belle holds against me.

ZADOK: Nonsense. You know what's a terrible thing? Self-pity,
        that's a terrible thing. Giving in, that's a terrible thing.
        Doing nothing, that's a terrible thing. Thinking the
        world's against you, that's a terrible thing. Not knowing
        that only you yourself is against you is a terrible thing.

IKE: You think that ending up here at the bottom of the
        world, a refugee, an immigrant, you think that was my
        doing?

ZADOK: It's irrelevant, Ike. It's not where you are it's *who* you
        are. Who you really are. You've been dealt a hand and
        all you're obliged to do is play the best game you can.
        That's all you can do, that's all any of us can do.

IKE: You mean to say, Zadok, a clever man like you, you
        mean to say that history, events not of our making,
        persecutions, wars, they don't make a mess of our lives?

ZADOK: Only if we let them.

IKE: You mean the Jews in Europe let the Nazis put them to
        death? You mean my grandfather allowed the Cossacks
        to behead him?

ZADOK: But you're not dead, Ike. You're alive and you had
        better live as though you're alive. And I speak as a dry,
        dusty, unemotional man.

IKE: I can't help feeling what I feel, Zadok —

ZADOK: [*exploding*] You can, you can help feeling what
        you feel, that's the whole point. We're not blighted,
        we're not cursed, we're not immobile, we have this
        ability to take our lives into our own hands, we can move
        or we can stand still, we can accept or we can reject, and
        we can *change*!

IKE: Zadok, give me a chance to explain. I can't help feeling
        that history spat me out here, that's what I feel —

ZADOK: All right, so it spat you out. History spits out people all
        the time. And some die, yes, and the world is cruel and
        relentless and savage. As I always say, there's no
        justice. But for those who live there's one obligation and
        that's life itself, Ike. Do me this favour, don't give into
        misfortune. At least do something about it. Let me
        make an appointment for you to see Norman Hurwitz —

IKE: I'll think about it

ZADOK: Please, I beg you, Ike, go and see him, and who knows?
        Your life could be transformed.

IKE: So, what else is new?

ZADOK: Things could be worse, Ike.

IKE: That's always true. But what about tomorrow, Zadok,

do you worry about the future?

ZADOK: I have my qualms. We've got a government here, they behave like Nazis, they *are* Nazis. Of course, I worry about the future —

IKE: You know what I say when I read about the government? I say thank God it isn't us they're picking on. It makes a nice change. Yes, the future, God help us.

ZADOK: Let me tell you something, Ike. You're blessed. And you know why? Because you have Leonard and Leonard is the future —

IKE: From your mouth into God's ear.

[*Silence.*]

Sometimes I feel I could do with procaine hydrochloride, an anaesthetic called Novocaine in 1905. One favour, Zadok, don't mention that psychiatrist to Belle —

ZADOK: If you'd rather I didn't —

[ZADOK *goes to* BELLE*'s door and opens it.*]

[*into the room*] I have to be going —

ROSE: [*off*] From 'Pippa Passes,' by Robert Browning.

ZADOK: Make it snappy.

ROSE: [*off*] 'From without is heard the voice of Pippa singing —

    The year's at the spring
    And day's at the morn;
    Morning's at seven;
    The hillside's dew-pearled;
    The lark's on the wing;
    The snail's on the thorn:
    God's in his heaven —
    All's right with the world!'

ZADOK: Touch wood. I'm off —

ROSE: [*off*) What time is it?

ZADOK: Quarter past.

ROSE: [*off*] I'm off, too —

BELLE: [*off*] Must you?

ROSE: [*off*] Yes, I must.

[ZADOK *withdraws, closing* BELLE*'s door.*]

ZADOK: So, Ike, you'll keep your promise?

IKE: What promise?

ZADOK: If I make an appointment for you to see Norman Hurwitz, you'll see him?

IKE: I made no promise. I'll think about it, that's what I promised. And that's what I'll do. I'll think about it. And Zadok, you can call in to see me without having a purpose, you take my meaning?

ZADOK: I take your meaning —

IKE: Because, for me, talking to you is better than listening to poetry.

[ROSE *comes out of* BELLE*'s room.*]

BELLE: [*off, calling*] Len, here a moment —

ROSE: Where's Leonard?

ZADOK: [*bellowing*] Leonard!

ROSE: So, Ike, did you have a nice chat with Zadok?

IKE: We had a chat.

ROSE: That's nice

[LEONARD *enters from the living room.*]

ZADOK: Leonard, your mother wants you. We're just off.

[LEONARD *tries to skirt past him.*]

Where you going? Don't I get a kiss?

[LEONARD, *reluctantly, goes to him.* ZADOK *stares at him for some seconds and smiles in a sickly way. Then, suddenly, he grabs* LEONARD*'s cheeks and squeezes them, making grunts of pleasure.*]

I love this boy.

[ROSE *kisses* LEONARD.]

ROSE: Goodnight, Len, Ike. See you soon. [*calling*] Goodnight, Belle —

ZADOK: Goodnight, Belle —

BELLE: [*off*] Goodnight —

[ZADOK *and* ROSE *exit.*]

[LEONARD *goes into* BELLE*'s room.* IKE *returns to his encyclopaedia.*]

[*off*] Ask your father if he wants cold chicken or eggs for supper.

[LEONARD *returns.*]

LEONARD: Dad, do you want cold chicken or eggs for supper?

IKE: Eggs.

LEONARD: [*to* BELLE *in her room*] Eggs. I'll have eggs, too.

[*He comes back into the hall, closing the door.*]

IKE: Len?

LEONARD: Yes?

IKE: Did you talk to your mother about what Professor Kinski said? About Vienna?

LEONARD: Yes.

IKE: What did she say?

LEONARD: She said she'd think about it.

[IKE *nods.* LEONARD *goes to his satchel and searches for a book.* IKE *stands for the first time. He drags his left leg and moves slowly across to* BELLE*'s door.* LEONARD *watches him.*

IKE *knocks on the door.*]

BELLE: [*off*] Who is it?

IKE: Me.

[*Silence.*]

[IKE *opens the door, goes into* BELLE'*s room and closes the door.*]

[LEONARD *stands perfectly still, waiting, in dread.*]

[*After a moment,* IKE *storms back into the hall.*]

God Almighty, God Almighty —

[*He sits at the table, angry, tormented.*]

[*shouting at* BELLE'*s room*] Why do you treat me like this? What have I done that's so terrible?

[*Silence.*]

[LEONARD *busies himself with his homework.*]

[*Lights fade to blackout.*]

SCENE TWO

BELLE'*s bedroom, just after 6.30 p.m., approximately the same time as the previous scene.*

The room is furnished with little taste. There is a single bed, a dressing table, an armchair, a built-in wardrobe and Degas prints of ballet dancers on the wall. The window has bars.

The door opens.

BELLE: [*off*] I'll be in my room —

LEONARD: [*off*] I won't be a moment —

ROSE: [*off*] Belle, you'll never guess what Ike just asked me —

BELLE: [*off*] That's true —

[BELLE *and* ROSE *enter.* BELLE *carries a tray with teapot and cups.*]

I wonder what Leonard wants to talk about. I'm always filled with such terrible foreboding —

[ROSE *sits.*]

ROSE: Listen to me, Belle, I think Ike's an amazing man —

BELLE: Yes, amazing.

ROSE: No, he is. I mean, he always knows what's going on. You know what he just asked me? About *The Naked and the Dead* —

BELLE: That American novel?

ROSE: Yes, filthy, you've no idea —

BELLE: Have you read it?

ROSE: Certainly. It's filth. Mind you, Belle, I laughed, there's one thing there, the soldier, when he hates someone, he puts them on what he calls his 'shit list'.
> [*They laugh.*]

Such words in a book —

BELLE: Has Ike read it?

ROSE: No, I told him not to. He's such an innocent, he wouldn't sleep for a week.

BELLE: He'd sleep. Ike sleeps through anything. Worse, he'd snore.

ROSE: How does Leonard cope with the snoring?

BELLE: He's like his father, he'll sleep through anything too. And when you're young —

ROSE: Sometimes I don't think it's right, a son shouldn't share a bedroom with his father.

BELLE: What d'you want me to do in a two-bedroom flat, you want me to sleep in the same room as Ike, you want me to be kept awake all night?

ROSE: Keep your hair on, Belle, I only said I wondered —

BELLE: I heard what you said. [*sits on the bed*] God, I'm tired. I'm tired of working.

ROSE: I brought something nice to read to you tonight.

BELLE: What?

ROSE: Robert Browning.

BELLE: Oh, my favourite.
> [*She rises and goes to the door.*]

What do they talk about, Leonard and his father?
> [*She opens the door a crack.*]

IKE: [*off*] — things like that are interesting. You should read these, Sir John Hammerton's Book of Knowledge, Leonard, I bought them for you —

BELLE: *I* bought them for him.
> [*She closes the door.*]

He bought them for him, he bought them for him —
> [*Silence.*]

ROSE: Belle, I want to talk to you.

BELLE: Talk.
> [*She sits down.*]

ROSE: About Ike.

BELLE: I don't want to talk about Ike, Rose.
> [*Silence.*]

ROSE: Zadok's going to be popping in this evening.

BELLE: Zadok, what for?

ROSE: He wants to have a word with Ike.

BELLE: I never understand our brother, Zadok. He's a highly intelligent man, Oxford-educated, what's he want to talk to Ike for?

ROSE: Ike's no fool. They were friends long before you married.

BELLE: Don't tell me, it was Zadok introduced us. So what's he want to talk to Ike about?

ROSE: I'm not going to make a secret of this, Belle. Zadok and I, we worry about you. And we worry about Ike.

BELLE: I worry about Ike, too.

ROSE: He's a decent man, Belle —

BELLE: Yes, decent —

ROSE: And he's not well, I mean the hand, the leg, his general health —

BELLE: Rose, I don't want to talk about it, really I don't.
[*Silence.*]

ROSE: Zadok ran into David Figg the other day, you remember David Figg, the doctor?

BELLE: Remember him? I knew him before he was born.

ROSE: People speak very highly of him. He's thought to be a top man.

BELLE: So?

ROSE: Well, he and Zadok met, they got to talking, one thing led to another, and they discussed Ike. David feels that Ike's problems are psychological —

BELLE: I could have told him that twenty years ago —

ROSE: He feels he should see a psychiatrist —

BELLE: From his mouth into God's ear.

ROSE: Listen, Belle, this is serious —

BELLE: I'm serious. I've always known my husband wasn't normal. At the age of forty-six his mother dies and he has a nervous breakdown, that's normal? I'll tell you one thing for certain, Rose, when I die he won't have a nervous breakdown.

ROSE: Zadok's going to talk to Ike tonight. He's going to suggest that Ike should see Norman Hurwitz.

BELLE: Who's he when he's at home?

ROSE: Norman Hurwitz? He's Professor of Psychiatry, the top man in the country, Belle.
[*Silence.*]

BELLE: How's the library?

ROSE: Can't complain. People are reading books. You'll

encourage Ike to see Norman Hurwitz, won't you, Belle?

BELLE: When's Zadok coming?

ROSE: Any time now.
[*Silence.*]

BELLE: I often wonder, Rose, how Ike and I ever produced someone like Leonard.

ROSE: You're not asking me, a spinster, to tell you about the facts of life, are you?

BELLE: [*smiling*] Shut up. I mean, when you think about it, Ike's such a peculiar man.

ROSE: Belle, these are the mysteries.
[*Silence.*]

BELLE: When I met Ike I thought he was the handsomest man I'd ever seen.

ROSE: And so he was, he was a wonderful looking man.

BELLE: He was doing so well then.
[*Silence.*]
I should have had Leonard earlier.
[*Silence.*]
Where does talent come from?
[*Silence.*]

ROSE: It's a shame he's an only child.
[*Silence.*]

BELLE: [*calling*] Leonard, come and talk to us, your maths can wait —
[*The front doorbell rings.* LEONARD *puts his head round the door.*]

LEONARD: There's someone at the door —
[*He goes.*]

BELLE: [*calling*] Leonard, is Uncle Zadok there?

LEONARD: [*off*] Yes, he's here —
[*A knock on the door.* ZADOK *puts his head in.*]

ZADOK: Sisters mine, it's your brudder.

BELLE: Hello, Zadok.

ROSE: Hello, Zadok.

BELLE: Tell Leonard to come and see me.

ZADOK: [*shutting the door*] Maestro, your mother wants to see you.

LEONARD: [*off*] Coming, Mom —

ROSE: That's good. Let Leonard be in here while Zadok talks to Ike.
[LEONARD *comes into the room.*]

BELLE: Have you finished your homework?

LEONARD: Nowhere near —

[ZADOK *puts his head round the door. He has a chicken leg in his hand.*]

ZADOK: I've stolen a chicken leg.

[*He disappears, closing the door.*]

BELLE: Sweetheart, come and sit, what did you want to tell me?

LEONARD: It can wait, Mom.

BELLE: No, it can't. I want to hear —

ROSE: You can tell her in front of me, Leonard, I'm family, remember?

LEONARD: All right, I'll tell you —

BELLE: Don't do us any favours.

LEONARD: I'll tell you. You asked me to tell you, I'll tell you.

BELLE: Leonard, you're not too old to be put across my knee and given a damn good hiding. Don't get short with me, get short with your father but not with me.

ROSE: All right, choose your weapons, seconds out, now let's behave like civilized human beings.

LEONARD: At my lesson today —

BELLE: Yes?

ROSE: With Professor Kinski?

LEONARD: [*irritated*] Yes —

BELLE: Leonard, relax, I can see you're tense, relax.

LEONARD: I'm trying to tell the story, you keep interrupting —

ROSE: Gong! Round two. Break clean, keep your punches above the belt, and come out talking.

BELLE: Rose, please. Go on, sweetheart —

LEONARD: He says, Professor Kinski says, he thinks I ought to go overseas to study. To Vienna, he says.

ROSE: Vienna, what's he talking about, Vienna, what's wrong with London?

BELLE: Rose, wait a moment. Tell me exactly what he said.

LEONARD: He said there was nothing more he could teach me.

ROSE: He said that?

LEONARD: Yes. He said — [*hesitates*]

ROSE: Tell us, don't be modest.

LEONARD: He said he'd never reached such a point with a pupil before. He said, he was so gentle today, he even wants to take me out to lunch in the holidays, he said he felt helpless. And Mom, I've been feeling for weeks now, he's got nothing more to teach me.

BELLE: You should have said, those lessons are costing me a fortune —

LEONARD: I know, I know, but what was I to do? Anyway, today he brought it up. He said I really need master classes and the only place I would find them is in Vienna, he said.

ROSE: The man's mad, who goes to Vienna nowadays? Only Graham Greene. And what would you learn in Vienna, the zither? You'll go to London —

BELLE: Rose, wait a moment. Leonard, look, I have to think —

LEONARD: Mom, I know, you don't have to explain —

BELLE: It's a big decision, a big trip, the cost, my God —

LEONARD: Look, I know, I mentioned it to Dad —

BELLE: You mentioned it to Dad, that'll be a great help —

ROSE: Can I ask a question? Everything's taken for granted in this household. I'd like to ask a basic question.

BELLE: Ask.

ROSE: Leonard, do you want to go overseas?
  [*Silence.*]
  Do you?

LEONARD: More than anything in the world.
  [BELLE *rises and pours herself another cup of tea.*]

ROSE: Do you want to go to Vienna?

LEONARD: I don't know where I want to go, I'd just like to go and study somewhere where I'd learn what I have to learn.

ROSE: That's settled, then.

BELLE: Rose, not so quick, it's not as simple as that.

ROSE: I'm not saying he's going tomorrow, Belle, I'm just establishing the young maestro's wishes in the matter.

LEONARD: I thought I might make some enquiries about New York —

ROSE: New York? What d'you mean, New York? You're another madman —

LEONARD: Aunty Rose, New York's a musical capital —

ROSE: Yes, like my left foot. What's wrong with London?

LEONARD: Nothing's wrong with London —

ROSE: Your Uncle Zadok, your mother and I were all born in London.

LEONARD: Aunty Rose, I know that, but it doesn't make London the musical capital of the world.

ROSE: What have got against London?

LEONARD: I've got nothing against London —

ROSE: Then what's all the talk about New York? And as for Vienna, I've never heard anything so ridiculous —

BELLE: Rose, Rose, wait a moment. Leonard, I have to think about this —

LEONARD: Of course.

BELLE: At this moment, I'm not so concerned about where you
         go —

ROSE: Belle, how can you say something like that? If he's
         going to go anywhere he's got to go to London —

BELLE: Rose, for God's sake, I've had a long day and now
         this to think about.

ROSE: Pardon me for breathing.

BELLE: Rose, look. Money doesn't grow on trees. Not in this
         house anyway. It's a big decision. I have to be certain I
         can afford his fare, the fees, his upkeep —

LEONARD: Mom, I know it's probably impossible. I just thought
         I'd better tell you —

BELLE: What d'you mean, impossible? I haven't said it's
         impossible, I just want to think about it —

LEONARD: If you say we can't afford it, I won't live the rest
         of my life eating my heart out.

         [*Silence.*]

ROSE: Leonard, I knew this day would come. I've thought
         about it often. I want you to develop not only into a great
         musician but also into a great artist. I want you to use
         London, I want you to — I argue it this way. London's
         the only place for you. London is the centre of the world.
         The most cultured people on earth gravitate towards
         London. They have the finest theatres in the world, the
         finest libraries. They have art galleries and concert
         halls. They have Winston Churchill and that gorgeous
         Anthony Eden. They have the finest system of
         government in the world. Did you know, Leonard, that
         in England when a Cabinet Minister leaves the presence
         of the King he has to walk backwards? Please God he
         should trip. What a system. And the King. And the
         Queen. And those two little darlings, Elizabeth and
         Margaret Rose. We are talking about a city, about
         Mecca, about Jerusalem, about London, about
         England. But you know above all what England has?
         England has English. Now, this is a language. Imagine,
         Leonard, if there'd been no pogroms. You know what
         you'd be talking now? Lithuanian. This is not a
         language. English is a language. And thank God for the
         Empire. Without the British Empire you'd be talking
         Zulu. How could you go to Vienna? What sort of
         language is German? It's a language for shouting
         orders. But English. Oh, Leonard, what a language.
         Take time to read, I beg you. Music may be your life,

Leonard, but, believe me, without books a person may as well be dead. You can keep your Russians, your Dostoevsky and Tolstoy, you can keep your French — Zola and Flaubert are good only for insomnia. But for life, Leonard, devour William Shakespeare, drink John Milton, taste Jane Austen, consume George Eliot, drown in Charles Dickens, glory in John Donne, whisper Wordsworth when you walk, befriend Robert Browning and let William Blake invade your dreams and nightmares. And if you are blue, I know you'll listen to the music that inspires you, but do me this favour: reach out for P.G. Wodehouse. Never mind he was a German spy, genius and decency don't always walk hand in hand — look at Wagner — but P.G. Wodehouse writes English to make Thomas Mann illiterate. I thank God that your mother, your Uncle Zadok and I were born in London. It's given us — it's given us culture. New York. Please. Americans are about as cultured as Miss Anna Katz. Have you read this man, Mailer?

LEONARD: No —

ROSE: Don't read him, Leonard, with his fug and fugging. Filth. But that's America. Norman Mailer. And to what American did they award a Nobel Prize for Literature? Pearl S. Buck, that's all they could find. Pearl S. Buck, I ask you. Mind you, she makes even Norman Mailer look as if he can write. No, no, Leonard. English. England. London. I want you to promise me you'll read, Leonard, you'll go to theatres and art galleries — and remember, always wear a tie when you go into the centre of London. It's the respect you pay a great city. And one more thing. How would you have managed in Vienna? At your school they don't teach languages, they teach Afrikaans. Afrikaans. Pearl S. Buck should have written in Afrikaans, it may have improved her style.

[*They laugh.* BELLE's *laughter turns to tears, which she tries to hide.*]

Belle, what's the matter —?

BELLE: What's the matter, what's the matter, what d'you think's the matter?

[*Silence.*]

LEONARD: Professor Kinski invited me to have lunch with him at the Waldorf.

ROSE: Well, it's better than having an enema but the results will be the same.

[BELLE *laughs.*]

LEONARD: He said he was very proud of me.

[*Silence.*]

I'll go and finish my homework and then I must practise.

ROSE: Uncle Zadok and your father may be talking privately. Be discreet.

BELLE: And Leonard —?

LEONARD: Yes?

BELLE: Give me a day or two —

LEONARD: There's no hurry —

BELLE: I've got a little saved, not much, I may be able to — I've just got to work it out. Just remember, everything happens for the best. I'm a fatalist. What will be, will be.

[LEONARD *opens the door to go.*]

ZADOK: [*off*] '— not in our stars but in ourselves,' ourselves, Ike, the fault is in us, in me, in you —

[LEONARD *goes, closing the door.*]

[*Silence.*]

BELLE: I've been dreading this moment ever since I can remember.

ROSE: I envy you.

BELLE: You need your head examined.

ROSE: To have a child like Leonard. To have a child who's —

[*She falls silent.*]

BELLE: I'll find a way, Rose, we won't talk about it, do you mind? I'll find a way, it's my responsibility.

ROSE: We'll all help —

BELLE: Certainly not —

ROSE: You're too proud, Belle, too proud.

BELLE: All right, so I'm too proud.

ROSE: We can all chip in.

BELLE: I won't have it.

ROSE: What do you mean you won't have it? It's only money we're talking about —

BELLE: Yes, only money —

ROSE: Belle, I know you haven't had it easy, but why make money such a big issue? Why let money ruin your life?

BELLE: [*turning on her*] How dare you, Rose? You don't know what it's like to lie awake night after night wondering where our next meal's coming from. Why let money ruin my life? Because money has ruined my life. All my contemporaries, without exception, have beautiful homes, comfortable lives. I'm nearly fifty, Rose, and I've had to go out to work every day for the last fifteen years.

I'm tired, I'm sick of it. You talk to me about Ike. He does nothing. He sits there, day after day, reading those encyclopaedias I bought for Leonard, without two pennies to rub together. He could get a job, he could do something, he does *nothing* to help, nothing. It all falls on me. It's fallen on me ever since the day his mother died and he went to pieces. It's fallen on me, the rent, the electricity, the maid, the food, Leonard's lessons, his pocket-money. When did I last have a new dress? When did I last go to the theatre or a film or a concert? What kind of life are we talking about?

ROSE: You've got Leonard.

BELLE: You didn't listen to a word I say, no one listens —

ROSE: Oh, I listen to you, Belle, I listen to every word you say. You've got Leonard, so stop feeling sorry for yourself. We're born into a world of indifference —

BELLE: Don't lecture me, please, Rose, you and Zadok, you lecture, you philosophise and I have to cope with the every-day, practical misfortunes —

ROSE: Belle, shut up and listen. I won't lecture you, I promise, but I'm going to tell you a story. Once upon a time —

BELLE: Rose, not now —

ROSE: Once upon a time, there was a young girl, thought by some to be a very beautiful young girl —

BELLE: Yes, very-beautiful-I-don't-think —

ROSE: Don't interrupt. And this beautiful young girl met a handsome young man. The two of them arrived at that moment in their lives at the end of a strange journey. He from Lithuania, which only the most generous-minded would call a country, and she from London —

BELLE: Yes, but of Polish parents, Rose, I've always thought it's because of my Slav temperament —

ROSE: She from London. By diverse routes, unlikely ever to have met if the world was a friendlier place, the two of them fall in love, yes, she falls in love. I remember, don't worry, I remember you writing 'Belle loves Ike' in the sands at Muizenberg and waiting for the sea to wash the words away. I remember. And this young girl and this young man marry. And very soon, for whatever reasons, no one except you and Ike can ever know, the romance turns sour. Even before Ike's mother died, there were problems. You don't have children —

BELLE: Rose, please —

ROSE: You're not going to shut me up, Belle, you're going to listen. All right. So, at last, they have a child, a son. And a year later, Ike's mother dies and he falls apart. His grief is too much for him to bear. Who knows why? A weakness, a sensitivity of which no one was ever aware, and people say it's not natural that a man in his mid-forties should grieve so for the loss of a mother. But it happens, and let me remind you that Hamlet, granted a much younger man than Ike, also grieved for the loss of a parent to the point of madness. So. It falls on the beautiful young girl to keep her family's body and soul together. That was what the Fates decreed. But there was compensation. At the age of five, the little boy, Leonard, goes to the piano in my flat above the library, I remember it as if it was yesterday, and he sits down and, instead of picking out *Three Blind Mice,* he plays a piece he heard on the wireless that morning, a minuet by Mozart. I don't believe in God, but that day was the nearest I came to it in my whole life. So, all right, being what I am, I settle for the Darwin view. By some accident of evolution, by some random disposition of the species, this couple, thrown together at the bottom of the world, produce a child of extraordinary gifts. And believe me, Belle, it's compensation for all the pain and misery and heartache. And something else. It placed on you an obligation which you took seriously and fulfilled to the last letter. You nurtured him, encouraged him, slaved for him. Now, he has to leave. He has to go out into the world so that the world can admire this accident of birth, this comet, this star. Nothing will stop it. Neither the lack of money nor the lack of will. It is inevitable. So, stop worrying. Take pleasure from your good fortune. Believe me, all will be well.

    [*Silence.*]

BELLE: I have to let him go, Rose. That's the pain. Not the struggle to send him on his way, but the letting go.

ROSE: I know, I know.

    [*Silence.*]

BELLE: Read me the Browning.

ROSE: Promise me you won't worry.

BELLE: I promise you I'll win the Irish Sweep.

    [ROSE *takes out a book of poetry.*]

ROSE: Robert Browning [*glances at her watch*] It'll have to be short.

BELLE: But not one of his love poems, Rose, something
        uplifting —
ROSE: All right, something to cheer you up —
        [ZADOK *puts his head round the door.*]
ZADOK: I have to be going —
        [ROSE *holds up her hand for him to be silent.*]
ROSE: From 'Pippa Passes' by Robert Browning.
ZADOK: Make it snappy.
ROSE: [*reading*] 'From without is heard the voice of Pippa
        singing —
                The year's at the spring
                And day's at the morn;
                Morning's at seven:
                The hillside's dew-pearled;
                The lark's on the wing;
                The snail's on the thorn:
                God's in his heaven —
                All's right with the world!'
ZADOK: Touch wood. I'm off —
ROSE: What time is it?
ZADOK: Quarter past.
ROSE: I'm off, too —
BELLE: Must you?
ROSE: Yes, I must.
        [ZADOK *withdraws.* ROSE *gathers her things.*]
        Maybe see you at the weekend, Belle —
BELLE: Bring the Browning again —
ROSE: [*kissing her*] Dont worry too much, Belle, though I know
        you, if there was nothing to worry about you'd worry
        there was nothing to worry about —
        [*She goes, leaving the door ajar.*]
BELLE: [*calling*] Len, here a moment —
ROSE: [*from the hall*] Where's Leonard?
ZADOK: [*off, bellowing*] Leonard!
ROSE: [*off*] So, Ike, did you have a nice chat with Zadok?
IKE: [*off*] We had a chat.
ROSE: [*off*] That's nice.
        [BELLE *takes knitting and a newspaper from her bag and
        starts to knit while reading.*]
ZADOK: [*off*] Leonard, your mother wants you. We're just
        off. [*Pause.*] Where you going? Don't I get a kiss.
        [*Pause. Then sounds of* ZADOK's *grunts of pleasure.*]
        [*off*] I love this boy.
BELLE: [*calling*] Leonard, where are you?

ZADOK: [*off*] Goodnight, I'm off

  ROSE: [*off*] Goodnight, Len, Ike. See you soon. Goodnight, Belle —

ZADOK: [*off*] Goodnight, Belle —

BELLE: Goodnight.

     [*After a moment,* LEONARD *enters.*]

     Ask your father if he wants cold chicken or eggs for supper.

     [LEONARD *stands in the doorway.*]

LEONARD: Dad, do you want cold chicken or eggs for supper?

  IKE: [*off*] Eggs.

LEONARD: [*to* BELLE *in her room*] Eggs. I'll have eggs, too.

     [*He goes, closing the door.*]

     [*Silence.* BELLE *knits and reads.*]

     [*After a moment a knock on the door.*]

BELLE: Who is it?

  IKE: [*off*] Me.

     [*Silence.*]

     [IKE *comes into the room and closes the door.*]

     Belle —

BELLE: What?

  IKE: Can you — can you lend me half-a-crown?

BELLE: Can I what?

  IKE: Half-a-crown, Belle, that's all, I'm broke, I want some cigarettes, I —

BELLE: I'm not a bank.

     [IKE *stands for a moment, trying to control his pain then turns and storms out of the room.*]

  IKE: [*off*] God Almighty, God Almighty — [*Pause, then, a shout:*] Why do you treat me like this? What have I done that's so terrible?

     [*Silence.*]

     [BELLE *knits.*]

     [*Lights fade to blackout.*]

SCENE THREE

The hall the moment the last scene ends.

IKE *has stormed back into the hall. He sits at the table, trying to calm himself.* LEONARD *is doing his homework.*

BELLE: [*off, calling*] Leonard. Here a moment.

           [LEONARD *rises and goes to the bedroom.*]

           [*off*] Give this to your father.

           [LEONARD *comes back into the hall without closing the door. He puts a coin on the table.*]

LEONARD: From Mom.

IKE: Len, do me a favour, pop down to the Greek shop and get me a packet of cigarettes —

BELLE: [*off*] Leonard, first you have to finish your homework and then practise —

LEONARD: No, no, I'll go now.

BELLE: [*off*] And close my door —

IKE: I'll do it, you get the cigarettes —

           [LEONARD *takes the coin and exits quickly.*]

           [BELLE *comes to her door.*]

BELLE: Leonard, close the door, were you born in a barn?

IKE: [*With difficulty*] Belle — Zadok's been talking to David Figg about me. David Figg, the doctor, a top man —

BELLE: I know.

IKE: You know? How do you know?

BELLE: How do I know? Rose told me, that's how I know.

IKE: You know about Hurwitz?

BELLE: About who?

IKE: About Hurwitz, the professor, the psychiatrist —

BELLE: Yes, I know about Hurwitz.

           [*Silence.*]

IKE: What you think?

           [*No response.*]

           Zadok's going to make an appointment for me.

           [*No response.*]

           What you think?

BELLE: [*intensely irritated*] About what?

IKE: Should I go and see the man?

BELLE: Do what you like.

IKE: I'm asking advice.

BELLE: I'm giving it.

IKE: I need some help —

BELLE: You need some help, what about me?

IKE: [*under his breath*] God Almighty —

BELLE: Yes, God Almighty —

           [*Silence.*]

IKE: Figg says my hand's mind over matter. You think it's possible?

BELLE: Yes, I think it's possible.

IKE: I want to use the hand.
[*Silence.*]
And there's Leonard, this overseas business —
BELLE: You leave Leonard to me —
IKE: Leave him to you, why should I leave him to you? I'm his father —
BELLE: Yes, yes, his father, some father —
IKE: Why should I leave him to you?
BELLE: Because —
IKE: Because what?
BELLE: Because, because —
IKE: Because what, because what?
BELLE: Because what else can you do about it?
IKE: What do you mean, what do you mean, what else can I do about it?
BELLE: You can do nothing about it except leave it to me —
IKE: I can do something about it, I can do something —
BELLE: What, what can you do?
IKE: I'll borrow —
BELLE: You'll borrow —
IKE: Yes, I'll borrow —
BELLE: From whom?
IKE: I'll find someone.
BELLE: Who'll lend you money?
IKE: I'll find someone —
BELLE: You'll find someone —
IKE: I'll borrow some money —
BELLE: Don't talk such nonsense, Ike —
IKE: I'll do it —
BELLE: Do it, do it, yes, do it —
IKE: I'll do it —
BELLE: You talk such nonsense —
IKE: He's my son —
BELLE: Yes, your son, your son —
IKE: I'll borrow some money —
BELLE: Leave me alone —
IKE: When I get the agency for the hangers —
BELLE: When, when, yes, when —
IKE: The plastic hangers, I'll turn the corner, even Zadok thinks so —
BELLE: Zadok, Zadok, what does Zadok know about plastic hangers —?
IKE: There's a fortune in plastic hangers —
BELLE: There was a fortune in Sir Seymour, there was a fortune

	in the fish shop —
IKE:	I'm talking about plastic hangers —
BELLE:	You're talking, you're talking, yes, talking.
	[*Silence.*]
	[IKE *shudders, trying to control tears.*]
IKE:	What did I do that was so terrible?
	[*No response.*]
	It's not a crime to go bankrupt.
	[*No response*]
	It wasn't my fault.
BELLE:	No, it was *my* fault.
IKE:	I didn't ask to go bankrupt
BELLE:	No, *I* asked for it.
IKE:	Shut up, Belle, shut up!
	[*Silence.*]
	[IKE *limps back to the table and is about to sit when* LEONARD *returns. He gives* IKE *a packet of ten cigarettes and the change.*]
	Give it to your mother, it's your mother's.
	[*While* IKE *lights a cigarette,* LEONARD *goes into the bedroom.*]
BELLE:	[*off*] I don't want it, let him have it —
	[LEONARD *comes back into the hall and puts the money on the table.* IKE *pockets it.*]
	[*off*] Lennie, were you born in a barn?
LEONARD:	What?
BELLE:	[*off*] Close my door.
	[LEONARD *goes to the door.*]
	[*off*] And, Leonard —
LEONARD:	What?
BELLE:	[*off*] Go and practise.
LEONARD:	I have to finish my homework first.
	[*He closes the door and goes back to the desk.*]
IKE:	Len —
LEONARD:	[*weary*] What, Dad?
IKE:	[*lowering his voice*] I owe you a couple of cigarettes.
LEONARD:	Dad, don't worry about it.
IKE:	I do worry about it, I always pay my debts.
LEONARD:	When I need, I'll ask.
IKE:	That's a deal.
	[BELLE *comes into the hall.*]
BELLE:	Leonard, don't you want supper?
LEONARD:	I'll make myself a sandwich later.
IKE:	I'll have a sandwich, too, Len can make me a sandwich, all right, Len?

LEONARD: Mom, Dad and I have been talking about my going overseas.

BELLE: That's nice for you.

LEONARD: I'm not absolutely certain about Vienna. As I said, I'm keen on New York, but Aunty Rose says London —

BELLE: Aunty Rose always says London.

IKE: We should take advice.

[LEONARD *sits at the table.*]

LEONARD: Yes, yes, I agree, that's right, we should take advice.

IKE: It's not what you know, it's who you know.

BELLE: And who do we know?

LEONARD: Well, I was thinking, there's Miss Katz —

IKE: Anna Katz?

BELLE: Anna Katz, Leonard, please —

LEONARD: Mom, she's a patron of the arts in Cape Town —

BELLE: With her money she can afford to be —

LEONARD: Everyone says she's very cultured —

BELLE: Cultured, Leonard, please, like my left foot she's cultured.

LEONARD: She came to my recital. She was very impressed.

BELLE: I didn't see her there —

[BELLE *sits at the table.*]

LEONARD: She told me I looked like Rachmaninoff.

IKE: Rachmaninoff? Rachmaninoff? What's she talking about, Rachmaninoff? He was bald.

LEONARD: She meant when he was young, Dad.

IKE: Rachmaninoff, you're nothing like Rachmaninoff. I've got pictures of him in Sir John Hammerton, Rachmaninoff looked like a pickled cucumber.

LEONARD: Not when he was young, Dad —

IKE: When he was young he looked like a young pickled cucumber. Rachmaninoff, the woman's mad. You're more like Ronald Colman.

BELLE: Don't be a bloody fool, Ike —

IKE: I'm telling you, he's more in the Ronald Colman style —

LEONARD: Ronald Colman's got a moustache.

IKE: Well, if he had one at your age he must have been very precocious, that's all I can say —

BELLE: Anyway, Ronald Colman's an actor.

IKE: Leonard can look like an actor —

BELLE: What's he want to look like an actor for?

IKE: It's not who he *wants* to look like, it's who he *does* look like. I'd like to look like King George VI, but I don't, so what can I do about it?

BELLE: [*laughing*] You talk such rubbish, Ike.

IKE: All I'm saying is, he can't help who he looks like. He could look like Winston Churchill, it's the luck of the draw.

BELLE: Winston Churchill —

IKE: People say I look like Walter Pidgeon —

BELLE: That I can see —

IKE: There you are, I look like an actor, why shouldn't my son look like an actor? And you, Belle, you look like the late Queen Alexandra, Edward VII's wife.

BELLE: I wish I had her money.

IKE: She was a beautiful woman, Belle. All I'm saying is, you can't help who you look like.

BELLE: I wish I did look like Queen Alexandra.

IKE: She was as deaf as a post.

LEONARD: Who was?

IKE: Queen Alexandra.

LEONARD: Was she, Dad?

IKE: Certainly.

BELLE: Was she, Ike?

IKE: The poor woman couldn't hear a fanfare from a full orchestra.

BELLE: Perhaps she didn't want to.

IKE: What are you saying, deafness can be mind over matter?

BELLE: Why not?
       [*Silence.*]

IKE: I've been meaning to say, Belle, you've got terrible rings under your eyes.

BELLE: I've got what?

IKE: Rings under your eyes, dark circles.

BELLE: Ike, are you feeling all right?

IKE: I'm fine, why?

BELLE: Because I've had these rings under my eyes for twenty-five years and it's the first time you've noticed them.

IKE: I've had other things to think about.
       [*A sort of laugh between them.*]
       Look, we're going to find a way, Leonard. God is good. He'll find a way. We're not in Pompeii —

BELLE: What are you talking about? What d'you mean we're not in Pompeii?

IKE: I'm talking about Pompeii and Herculaneum. We can't sit here worrying about volcanic eruptions. We just have to believe that things get better not worse. Perhaps Zadok's right. Perhaps it's up to us. I don't know.

Sometimes I'm full of hope, other times I'm in Pompeii and Herculaneum. Anyway, get rid of those shadows, Belle, sleep easy, we'll find a way.

[*Silence.*]

LEONARD: I could work for a year

BELLE: What?

LEONARD: After I've done my matric, I could work for a year, save as much as possible, that'd help, wouldn't it?

BELLE: How much d'you think you'd earn?

LEONARD: I don't know, twenty, thirty pounds a month, I could save half, that'd help —

IKE: Nonsense, nonsense, I'll work —

BELLE: Ike, please —

IKE: I'll work —

BELLE: Ike, you haven't worked for two, three, four years —

IKE: I'll find a job —

BELLE: You say that —

IKE: I mean it —

BELLE: What kind of job — ?

IKE: I don't know —

BELLE: What's there for you to do?

IKE: I'll work, I'll work —

BELLE: Yes, yes, you'll work —

IKE: Give me another week, I'll know about the plastic hangers —

BELLE: Plastic hangers —

IKE: Give me a week —

BELLE: Give you a week, I've given you twenty-five years —

IKE: I'm asking for a little time, a week, that's all, maybe ten days, I'm waiting to hear, it's not my fault.

BELLE: Not your fault, not your fault, whose fault is it, mine? If it's not your fault I'd like to know whose fault it is —

LEONARD: Please, please —

BELLE: Leonard, don't interfere —

IKE: I've had bad luck, that's all, I've had some bad luck —

BELLE: Other people have bad luck, it seems to change, your bad luck lasts a lifetime —

[LEONARD *goes into the sitting room.*]

IKE: [*without pause*] It's only been difficult since the war —

BELLE: It was difficult before the war, that's when you had the nervous breakdown, before the war —

IKE: My mother died, Belle —

BELLE: You won't have a nervous breakdown when I die.

IKE: I've had my troubles —

BELLE: You're telling me —
        [*In the living room* LEONARD *starts to play the piano loudly
        and furiously: Rachmaninoff's Prelude, Opus 3, No. 2.*]
        [*In the hall,* IKE *and* BELLE *instinctively raise their voices.*]
IKE: It wasn't my fault I went bankrupt —
BELLE: You've been bankrupt all your life —
IKE: You've got no pity —
BELLE: No one's got any pity —
IKE: What did I do that's so terrible? I keep asking the
        question but I don't get the answer. What did I do?
BELLE: It's what you didn't do —
IKE: Where's your pity, then, where's your pity?
BELLE: Pity for what, pity for who?
IKE: For me, for me, I'm a sick man, yes, pity for me —
BELLE: For you? For you? Pity for you?
IKE: Yes, for me, for me, pity for me —
BELLE: Me, me, me, me, me, me, me —
        [*There is a banging on the ceiling, which they ignore.*]
IKE: Belle, the world hasn't treated me well —
BELLE: Oh, shut up, shut up, for God's sake, shut up, the
        world, me, but never you, Ike, never you —
IKE: I was given a hand with fours high —
BELLE: Given what, a hand with what, given what?
IKE: Fours high, fours high —
BELLE: Fours high, fours high, you're mad, what are you
        talking about, fours high, your mind's disturbed —
IKE: My mind, my mind —
BELLE: Zadok's right, you should see a psychiatrist, go and
        see a psychiatrist —
IKE: Why don't you go and see a psychiatrist? You're also
        in need of treatment —
BELLE: You can always divorce me —
IKE: Divorce you, yes, divorce you —
        [*More banging on the ceiling.*]
        — and what about Leonard? How can I divorce you
        when we've got a child like Leonard?
        [BELLE *storms into her room.*]
        [LEONARD *continues to play the piano in the living room.*]
        [IKE *sits at the table and then suddenly starts to have difficulty
        breathing. He tries to calm down but gasps noisily, like awful
        moans. He tries to stand but can't.*]
        [*The music continues.*]

[*At last* IKE *manages to stand. He staggers to* BELLE'S *bedroom door.*]

Belle —

[*He collapses.* BELLE *opens her door.*]

BELLE: [*almost a scream*] **Ike!**

[*She goes to him.*]

Ike, what is it — ?

IKE: **I can't — I can't — catch my — my breath —**

BELLE: [*a scream*] **Leonard!**

[*The music continues.*]

[*louder*] **Leonard!**

[*The music continues.*]

[*shouting*] **Leonard, come quickly —**

[LEONARD *comes into the hall.*]

Get a doctor, run to the corner, get Dr. Simons —

LEONARD: **What's happened, what's the matter with Dad?**

BELLE: **Just go —**

[LEONARD *runs from the house.*]

[IKE *hyperventilates.*]

The doctor's coming, Ike, the doctor's coming —

IKE: **I can't — I can't — I can't —**

BELLE: **Don't try to speak, don't try to speak —**

IKE: [*with enormous effort; staccato*] **I'm not — I'm not — I'm trying — to catch — my breath —**

[BELLE *watches over him.*]

[*Lights fade to blackout.*]

SCENE FOUR

A week later. Night.

BELLE *and* LEONARD *are sitting in* BELLE'S *bedroom. The mirrors are covered.*

BELLE: **Doctors. What do they know? Meningioma. Sounds like something a poet should die from. Meningioma. Shall I read what David Figg says? A G.P. A top man.**

[*She picks up a letter.*]

[*reading.*] **'Meningioma means a tumour growing along the blood vessels on the surface of the brain. It can be either malignant or benign. In your late husband's case, the tumour was benign. We know very** little about such growths. The pathologist is of the opinion that the tumour had been present for several years but that its development was erratic. For long periods it would, apparently, lie dormant and then, due perhaps to some emotional or physical disturbance, become active, causing slow progressive damage to the brain. What is puzzling is that Mr. Lands did not suffer unduly from the symptoms one would normally expect, such as severe headaches or convulsive seizures. I hope all of this is of some help. I wish you and your son long life. David Figg.'

[*Silence.*]

Meningioma. And David Figg was the doctor who said mind over matter. Doctors. What do they know?

[*Silence.*]

You know the worst two words in the English language, Leonard, in any language? 'If only.'

[*Silence.*]

It makes me laugh. Everything these days is psychology. Everybody's blaming their parents or their nannies, everybody's suffering from an unhappy childhood or some shock to their system they can't talk about until Freud interprets their dreams and life is suddenly bearable again Everybody's haunted by their own past. Trust Ike to be different. With Ike it was never just one thing. With him it couldn't just be mind over matter, it couldn't just be a growth on the brain, it had to be both. Such a complex man. Meningioma. 'If only.'

[*Silence.*]

Leonard, I wish you'd cry, I'm stifled with foreboding.

[*Silence.*]

I should have known he was seriously ill when he mentioned the shadows under my eyes. Twenty-five years of marriage and the first time he says anything about my eyes is on the day he dies.

[*Silence.*]

I'm not going to be haunted. I'm not going to ruin the rest of my life with guilt. I'm not going to apologise. We fought. We argued. I'm a difficult woman. He was a difficult man. I'm not going to lie. We only fought about one thing. Perhaps money was a symbol, who knows?

[*Silence.*]

I can't weep either. But that's all right. I've seen those widows at their husbands' funerals, they throw themselves into the grave, weep and wail and tear their hair out. They're always the quickest to remarry.

[*Silence.*]

I'm never going to lie about Ike and me. I won't bathe his memory in sunshine.

[*Silence.*]

The past is the past. What will be, will be. I'm a fatalist. We have to make plans, Leonard. We have to think only of the future, your future. You'll go overseas, Vienna, London, New York, wherever. Don't worry, somehow you'll go. If I have to eat one meal a week, you'll go. I'll work to the end of the chapter. As long as there's a purpose I don't mind. Because, to tell you the truth, Leonard, there's nothing else I care about except your future. Not now. I always thought when I had you that I couldn't be alone ever again. Well, one can always be wrong. I have total confidence in you, I believe in your gifts, I have absolute faith. You're my future, Leonard. The past can go to hell.

[*Silence.*]

[*Lights fade to blackout.*]

END OF ACT ONE

ACT TWO

Thirty-five years later.

The studio and control booth of a recording studio in Maida Vale, London.

The studio is dominated by a grand piano. There are microphones on stands; others are suspended. Music stands. Chairs. A door to a corridor, which leads to the outside world and to the control booth, which is separated from the studio by a large sound-proof window and is fitted with a console and a bank of sound-mixing equipment, amplifiers, speakers. Chairs at the console. Behind the main control area is space with chairs.

SCENE ONE

Just after 1 p.m.

The sound of a Rachmaninoff prelude over the speakers.

A dim light on TWO TECHNICIANS *in the control booth.*

In the studio, LEONARD, *now 51, listens and makes notes on a printed manuscript.*

Into the control booth comes JEREMY LANDS, *aged 18, smart, contemporary, trendy. He is, however, deeply unconfident and easily embarrassed by himself and others. He sees* LEONARD *in the studio. He asks permission of the* TECHNICIANS *then switches a switch on the console.*

JEREMY: [*through the loudspeaker*] Dad — ? Dad —?
      [LEONARD *jumps with fright then sees* JEREMY.]
LEONARD: [*into a microphone*] Jeremy! What are you trying to do? Give me a heart attack?
JEREMY: They're here, is it all right to bring them in?
LEONARD: Have they had lunch?
JEREMY: Yes.
LEONARD: Where are they?
JEREMY: In the corridor. I thought I'd better check —
TECHNICIAN: Shall we take lunch now, Maestro?
LEONARD: Yes, back in an hour.
      [*The* TWO TECHNICIANS *leave.*]

[ROSE, *now 86, and* ZADOK, *89, enter.* ROSE, *a little hard of hearing, and* ZADOK, *who walks on two sticks, enter the control booth.*]

ROSE: Where is he, I could hear Leonard's voice, where is he?

LEONARD: [*through the speaker*] I'm in the studio, Aunty Rose —

ZADOK: [*confused*] Where, where, where — ?

JEREMY: [*pointing*] He's in there —

ROSE: There he is!

[*They stand at the window, waving to him.* LEONARD *waves back.*]

LEONARD: Jeremy, bring them round —

[JEREMY *ushers* ROSE *and* ZADOK *out of the booth.* LEONARD *goes to the studio door and opens it for them. He kisses* ROSE *and goes to to kiss* ZADOK *but* ZADOK *grabs his cheeks and squeezes them with grunts of pleasure.*]

Where's Mom?

ROSE: She's gone where you can't go for her.

LEONARD: Jeremy, go and wait for Granny. I don't want her to get lost.

[JEREMY *goes.*]

ZADOK: Don't worry about her. Belle doesn't get lost that easily. Independent? I've never known a woman like it. I should be so independent. But what can I do with these sticks? I should stick them, that's what I should do, I should stick these sticks where the monkey sticks his nuts.

[*He laughs.*]

ROSE: Ignore him, he's ga-ga.

ZADOK: I've got to sit down. Can I sit in this chair?

LEONARD: Sit anywhere —

ZADOK: All right, I'll sit on the floor.

[*He laughs and sits on a chair.*]

ROSE: [*a warning*] Len, you have to tell your mother. You know what I'm talking about.

ZADOK: What's going on, what's going on, what's the big secret?

ROSE: You know the secret, Leonard told me in absolute confidence yesterday, and I told you last night. Now Len's got to tell Belle.

ZADOK: Me, I don't give a damn what you do, Len. But remember this: there's no justice in this world.

LEONARD: As my father used to say.

ZADOK: Ike never said anything like that in all his life. All Ike knew was God is good. And that he got wrong.

LEONARD: So, did you have a good morning?

ROSE: Fish and chips.

ZADOK: You have to shout, she's as deaf as a post.

LEONARD: Did you have a good morning?

ROSE: You know where we went?

LEONARD: Where?

ROSE: To Stepney. To see the house where we were born, the three of us.

ZADOK: Only it wasn't there.

LEONARD: Couldn't you find it?

ZADOK: How can you find a house that's been bombed to bits? The Germans bombed our house. They were totally indiscriminate. I almost wept, me, a dry, dusty, unemotional man. And what they've put up in its place, you can't imagine. Sometimes I think Hitler won the war. What they've done to London, it looks like Albert Speer designed the buildings. You know who Albert Speer was?

LEONARD: Hitler's architect.

ROSE: Of course he knows who Albert Speer was. Leonard reads books. He's cultured. [again, the warning] You must talk to your mother, Len, otherwise there'll be hell to pay.

LEONARD: Yes, yes, I will.

ROSE: Where is she? She said she was going to the lavatory.

ZADOK: Perhaps she didn't mean in this building, perhaps she meant in Timbuctoo.

ROSE: Ignore him, he's ga-ga.

ZADOK: And when are we going to see you properly, Leonard? We've been here two days, we've hardly talked —

ROSE: He's a busy man, Zadok, a famous man —

ZADOK: So famous men talk to their relations, don't they, how else do you explain nepotism?

LEONARD: Tomorrow, I promise, I've kept the whole morning free. You'll come to the flat and we'll talk. Jeremy will drive you.

ROSE: Thank you, I'd rather take a taxi. That Jeremy of yours drives like he's on the dodgems. But what a beautiful boy, I could eat him. What's he going to do with his life — ?

ZADOK: God forbid he wants to be a chauffeur —

ROSE: Is he still so keen on the theatre? Stella said his heart was set on becoming an actor —

LEONARD: You ask him, Aunty Rose, he doesn't tell me anything. He's extremely bright and extremely obstinate.

ZADOK: Leonard, you still see Stella?

ROSE: Zadok, don't be so tactless —

[BELLE, *aged 84, enters with* JEREMY. *She has aged well, is smartly dressed, well-groomed.* LEONARD *kisses her.*]

LEONARD: All right, Mom?

BELLE: Never better.

ZADOK: We thought you got flushed down the toilet.

BELLE: Ignore him, he's ga-ga.

ZADOK: What about me? Why don't I get a kiss? Have I got impetigo or something?

ROSE: You've had a kiss.

ZADOK: When, when, when did I have a kiss?

ROSE: Leonard, do me this favour, kiss Zadok again or he'll drive us all mad.

[LEONARD *leans over to kiss* ZADOK, *who squeezes his cheeks and grunts.*]

LEONARD: [*to* BELLE] So, I hear you couldn't find the house.

BELLE: Would you believe it? The Germans bombed it.

ROSE: I was telling Len we couldn't find the house.

BELLE: She's as deaf as a post. She only hears what she shouldn't hear.

ROSE: What time does the recording start? I'm so excited, I've never been in a recording studio before —

LEONARD: At about two. The technicians are having lunch. I've only one more prelude to do.

BELLE: Rachmaninoff?

LEONARD: Yes.

BELLE: [*to* ROSE *proudly*] He's going to record one more Rachmaninoff prelude. I'm sick to death of listening to you on records, Leonard, I want to hear you in the flesh for a change. When you play in Cape Town next year, you must play Rachmaninoff.

ZADOK: [*disparaging*] British workmen.

ROSE: What are you talking about, Zadok?

ZADOK: The technicians. British workmen. Never finish a job.

ROSE: They've got to eat, Zadok.

ZADOK: Why?

ROSE: [*a loud whisper, to* LEONARD] Please talk to your mother, Leonard. You've got to tell her.

BELLE: What's going on, what's he got to tell me?

LEONARD: And you, Uncle Zadok, I hear you've moved into the Old Aged Home. Are you comfortable there?

ZADOK: Who says?

LEONARD: I'm asking.

ZADOK: I'm comfortable, but have you tried talking to old people? You think Rose is deaf —

ROSE: Who says I'm deaf?

BELLE: You see, what she shouldn't hear she hears.

ZADOK: We've got one fellow there, Abe Bendel, this man couldn't hear a baboon fart two feet away —

BELLE: Zadok —

ZADOK: I'm telling you. He gives us all laryngitis.

LEONARD: But you're happy there.

ZADOK: Happy. Yes, I'm happy. Every morning I wake up, I jump out of bed, I dance the sailor's hornpipe, I sing the Hallelujah Chorus, I open the windows, I shout out, 'I'm so happy here in the Old Aged Home,' me, a former Professor of Moral Philosophy, a dry, dusty, unemotional man, I'm so happy I'm singing, I'm dancing, 'Hal-le-lu-jah.'

BELLE: Oh, shut up, Zadok, you get on my nerves, you're about as dry and dusty as a tragedy queen.

LEONARD: And Aunty Rose, you still live above the lending library?

ROSE: If I wasn't near my books I'd die.

ZADOK: So, instead of a shroud they'll wrap you in a dust jacket.

ROSE: [*her loud whisper*] Leonard, you've got to tell your mother —

BELLE: Rose, if you whisper any louder you may as well shout. What have you got to tell me, Leonard? Is it bad news? [*genuinely anxious*] Aren't you well?

LEONARD: I'm fine, it can keep, so what's all the Sea Point gossip?

ZADOK: Stand by, here comes the obituary column.

ROSE: Poor Miss Anna Katz died.

ZADOK: What did I tell you?

LEONARD: I'm sorry, what was wrong with her?

ZADOK: She was ninety, that's what was wrong with her.

BELLE: [*mouths the word*] Cancer.

LEONARD: What?

BELLE: [*again mouthing the word*] Cancer.

ZADOK: Cancer, cancer, say it, you're not going to catch it from saying it. Cancer. It's a perfectly healthy disease.

ROSE: A healthy disease, he's ga-ga.

BELLE: Leonard, what is it you're supposed to tell me?

LEONARD: Miss Anna Katz, Jeremy, was extremely kind to me when I was young. She arranged a big farewell benefit concert for me in Cape Town. They raised a lot of money. Without her I couldn't have gone overseas.

ROSE: Never mind Miss Katz, without your mother you couldn't have gone overseas.

BELLE: And she was so looking forward to your welcome back concert next year. The last time I saw her that's all she talked about. A week later —

ROSE: Well, that's life, Belle.

ZADOK: No, Rose, that's death.

BELLE: Leonard, I'm filled with foreboding. I've been filled with foreboding all my life. I always expect something terrible to happen. I'm always on edge, minute by minute, hour by hour, day by day, I think the world's going to explode. I can't bear it. I want to know what's going on.

LEONARD: Tell you what, come through with me into the control booth, we can talk there. Come on, Mom. Jeremy, you look after Uncle Zadok and Aunty Rose.

[*He leads* BELLE *out.*]

ROSE: She's going to have a nervous breakdown, I'm telling you.

ZADOK: Listen, Belle doesn't have nervous breakdowns, that was Ike's department.

ROSE: He should have told her right away.

JEREMY: Yes, but Dad's a coward.

[*An awkward silence.* LEONARD *and* BELLE *appear in the booth and they sit.* ROSE, ZADOK *and* JEREMY *watch them.*]

ROSE: Life's funny.

ZADOK: I'm not laughing.

ROSE: Look at them, mother and son. Your grandmother, Jeremy, sacrificed everything for your father. Everything. And now he's going to break her heart.

ZADOK: You read too many novels, Rose. Belle sacrificed nothing. She did what she wanted to do. And she's got a heart like a rock. She'll live forever. And don't get sentimental. I can't bear sentimentality.

ROSE: She seems to be taking it well.

JEREMY: He hasn't told her yet.

ROSE: How do you know?

JEREMY: I know.

[*In the booth,* LEONARD *swtiches a switch.*]

LEONARD: Mom wants to say something.

ROSE: Oh my God, here it comes —

LEONARD: Speak, Mom, they can hear now —

BELLE: I've got this to say. Stop staring at us. You're making me feel as though I'm in a goldfish bowl. [*to* LEONARD] They won't take any notice, Rose probably didn't even hear me, in five minutes she'll be looking again, nosy —

[LEONARD *switches the switch. He and* BELLE *continue to talk.*]

ROSE: Belle's such a difficult woman.

ZADOK: Talking of difficult women, how's your mother, Jeremy? How's Stella?

JEREMY: Fine.

ROSE: Stella was never difficult, Stella was an angel. I'd love to see her again. You remember when you visited us in Cape Town, Jeremy? What a time we had —

ZADOK: How could he remember? He was three years old —

ROSE: I'd really love to see Stella again.

ZADOK: So would I, what a girl, what a figure.

JEREMY: She said she'd like to see you, but —

ZADOK: And fair hair, I've never seen such fair hair. A suicide blonde. Dyed by her own hand.

[*He laughs.*]

ROSE: Stella never dyed her hair. She was a natural blonde. How can you say such a thing?

ZADOK: It's a joke, an old joke, can't a man make an old joke?

ROSE: And the most beautiful complexion I've ever seen. Peaches and cream, a real English beauty.

ZADOK: No one's got any sense of humour any more.

ROSE: The Honourable Mrs Leonard Lands, what a ring that had to it —

ZADOK: What's she talking about now?

ROSE: I'm talking about Stella. She's an Honourable. Her father's a Lord —

ZADOK: I know, I know, my memory's unimpaired, unlike your hearing —

ROSE: The Mitfords were all Honourable. They had a cupboard. The Hons cupboard.

ZADOK: What are you talking about, Honourable? One of them was Hitler's popsy. She had a funny name.

ROSE: Unity.

ZADOK: Unity, what a name. She was a Nazi, she should've stayed in the cupboard. And one of them married Mosley, what's so Honourable about them?

ROSE: It's a title, Zadok. [*to* JEREMY] Please, ignore him.

ZADOK: I don't see why we can't see Stella. Just because they're divorced, it doesn't mean we can't see her.

[ROSE *looks into the booth.*]

ROSE: You think he's told her yet?

JEREMY: No. He's still looking at her. You'll know when he tells her. When he turns his back. Dad never looks at you when he's got something unpleasant to say.

[*An awkward silence.*]

ZADOK: I'll tell you something in confidence, Jeremy. Your father, he was always a secretive boy.

ROSE: He's an artist. All artists are secretive.

ZADOK: Listen, you want my candid opinion, I always thought Leonard was a little bit wet.

ROSE: What are you talking about? You adored him, you still adore him —

ZADOK: You can adore someone who's wet.

ROSE: Please don't talk like this in front of Jeremy. It's not seemly.

ZADOK: Nonsense. He's family. In a family everything's seemly.

ROSE: Your father came to England when he was seventeen, Jeremy, —

JEREMY: I know —

ROSE: — all on his own, his mother let him go, just like that, at seventeen, he was still wet behind the ears, but he coped, he managed and he's had a wonderful career, a wonderful life. Even my hairdresser's heard of Leonard Lands. They buy his records, we're talking about a leading musician, our Leonard, just imagine.

ZADOK: When your father was a boy, Jeremy, you never knew what he was thinking. He never said much. Always very quiet, docile. Cowed. That's the word I want, cowed. And very hard to get at.

JEREMY: That's still true.

ROSE: He's an artist, a musician, a pianist. A pianist doesn't have to think, he doesn't have to speak, he doesn't have to be noisy. All a pianist has to do is play the piano and that Leonard does divinely.

ZADOK: [*to* JEREMY] In her eyes your father can do no wrong.

ROSE: He's given me more pleasure than any other human being I've ever known.

ZADOK: What she shouldn't hear she hears —

ROSE: He's also the pride of Belle's life and that's why I'm so concerned that when he tells her — God knows what it'll do to her.

ZADOK: I'll tell you the trouble with your father, Jeremy. He bottles things up inside.

JEREMY: That's what the doctor said after his breakdown.

[*Shocked silence.*]

ROSE: Whose breakdown?

JEREMY: Dad's.

ROSE: When? When did he have a breakdown?

JEREMY: Five years ago, just after Mummy left him.

ZADOK: Did he have an X-ray?

JEREMY: No, Uncle Zadok, it was a breakdown. You don't have an X-ray for a breakdown.

ZADOK: In this family you do.

ROSE: Zadok, you're not to mention this to Belle. Why weren't we told? Stella should have told us, someone —

ZADOK: How is he now?

JEREMY: I don't know, I don't see very much of him any more. And when we meet all we seem to do is row.

[*Silence.*]

[*In the booth,* LEONARD *stands and turns his back on* BELLE.]

He's telling her now.

[*They watch.*]

ZADOK: Cramp! I've got cramp. I've got to stand. Jeremy, help me —

[JEREMY *helps* ZADOK *to stand.* ZADOK *stamps his feet.*]

ROSE: Are you all right? We walked too much this morning, are you all right?

ZADOK: It'll go, it'll go —

[ROSE *rushes to the window.*]

ROSE: [*yelling at* BELLE *and* LEONARD] It's only cramp! It'll go!

JEREMY: Aunty Rose, they can't hear you —

ROSE: [*yelling*] It's only cramp!

ZADOK: Don't shout at me, I know it's cramp. I'm not deaf, I know it'll go —

[LEONARD *and* BELLE *have noticed the fuss in the studio.* LEONARD *switches a switch.*]

LEONARD: What's the matter?

ROSE: [*yelling*] Zadok's got cramp!

BELLE: I thought he was having a heart attack.

ZADOK: It's gone. It's all right. Don't make such a fuss. I'm fine.

ROSE: [*to the booth, yelling*] He's fine.

BELLE: I can hear, thank you.

ROSE: He's as fit as a fiddle.

ZADOK: From your mouth into God's ear.

ROSE: [*whispering*] Everything all right, Belle?

BELLE: [*to* LEONARD] She doesn't realise the microphone's on.

[LEONARD *switches the switch but* BELLE *goes on talking to* ROSE *who, of course, can't hear*.]

ROSE: I can't hear! I can't hear!

[BELLE *has a word with* LEONARD, *who switches the switch again*.]

BELLE: — the switch.

LEONARD: It's on.

BELLE: You're sure?

LEONARD: Yes, I'm sure.

BELLE: All right, then. [*to the studio*] Please leave us in peace, my son and I are having a private conversation.

[LEONARD *switches the switch*. ZADOK *sits*. BELLE *and* LEONARD *continue to talk in the booth*.]

ROSE: You all right, Zadok?

ZADOK: How do I look?

ROSE: You look all right.

ZADOK: Then why ask?

[*Silence*. ROSE *looks into the booth*. BELLE *sees her and waves her away*.]

ROSE: I don't think she's taking it well.

[*Silence*.]

ZADOK: Jeremy, this breakdown your father had, was he very ill?

JEREMY: I think so. He couldn't play for three or four months.

ROSE: Why, was there something wrong with his hands, why, why, why couldn't he play?

JEREMY: I don't know —

ROSE: Stella was right not to tell Belle.

[*Silence*.]

It's like music.

ZADOK: What's like music?

ROSE: Life. Life's like music.

ZADOK: Rose, I'm the philosopher. You leave life to me. I'll leave art to you.

ROSE: If we left life to philosophers there'd be no art. Life is like music.

ZADOK: She's going to tell us whether we want to hear or not.

ROSE: You have themes, variations, movements, motifs, developments, resolutions —

ZADOK: What are you talking about, resolutions, what resolutions? In life nothing is ever resolved —

ROSE: Take the whole business with Ike. His illness. His

tumour and his state of mental health. Think of it as a
theme. Now Leonard plays a variation.

ZADOK: And she says I'm ga-ga. And you, Jeremy, what
variations are you going to play?

JEREMY: I don't know.

ZADOK: They tell me you're very bright.

ROSE: You still want to be an actor?

ZADOK: How can he be very bright and still want to be an actor?

ROSE: The last time Stella wrote to me she said you wanted to
be an actor.

JEREMY: I don't know now. I don't know whether to be an actor or
a merchant banker.

ROSE: Are you serious?

JEREMY: Yes. I think nowadays one needs to make money
young —
          [*He becomes embarrassed.*]

ROSE: That's a choice? An actor or a merchant banker?

ZADOK: Be a merchant banker. It's more precarious.
          [*He laughs.*]

ROSE: What does your mother say?

JEREMY: She says I must make up my own mind. I don't think she
really cares —

ROSE: Of course she cares. And your father, what's his opinion?

JEREMY: I haven't discussed it with him.

ZADOK: You and Leonard are not close?

JEREMY: No.

ZADOK: So, Rose, what kind of variation is that? You see,
Jeremy, Leonard and his father were like that —
          [*He crosses his fingers.*]

ROSE: You talk such nonsense, Zadok. Lennie and Ike hardly
ever exchanged three words consecutively.

ZADOK: Never mind, I always had the feeling they were thick as
thieves. There was something between them. An
unspoken understanding. I would say they were close.

ROSE: You would say, you would say, take no notice of him,
Jeremy, he's ga-ga.

JEREMY: My father and I have never exchanged more than three
words consecutively. He disapproves of me. I
disapprove of him.

ROSE: Jeremy, that's a terrible thing to say —

JEREMY: It's true.

ZADOK: What do you disapprove of? Don't you like the way he
plays the piano?

JEREMY: My father wants to be loved too much.

ZADOK: Who doesn't? Let me tell you, Jeremy, my wife died after we were married three months, and —
[*He shudders with tears.*]

ROSE: All right, Zadok, all right —

ZADOK: [*still shuddering*] It's not all right, it's not all right, it's not such a terrible thing to want to be loved.

JEREMY: [*gaining confidence*] But Dad doesn't want to be loved by me or by Mummy, he wants to be loved by the world. He wants to be thought well of. He wants not only to be on the right side, but also to be seen to be on the right side.

ZADOK: This boy *is* bright.

JEREMY: It's not enough for him to be a wonderful pianist, he has to be a public figure, sign petitions, march, support causes —

ZADOK: And you don't? You don't support causes? I thought all young people these days supported causes.

JEREMY: Only after I've made up my own mind.

ZADOK: That sounds smug, oh God, does that sound smug.

JEREMY: [*embarrassed*] I'm sorry. That's what I feel. That's why I've decided to visit South Africa —

ZADOK: You're coming to South Africa? When? You hear that, Rose? Jeremy is coming out to South Africa.

ROSE: What? What? I haven't been following, I thought he said he wasn't coming to South Africa —

ZADOK: No, Jeremy, Jeremy's coming to South Africa —

ROSE: Jeremy! When, when are you coming, when?

JEREMY: When I've saved enough —

ROSE: What d'you mean, saved enough? Isn't your father paying? He can afford it —

JEREMY: He's matching me pound for pound —

ZADOK: Another merchant banker —

JEREMY: I'm working at night in a restaurant and saving all I can. Dad doesn't want me to go. He says I'm doing it for spite. He may be right. But what he actually thinks is that it'll reflect badly on him. I know my father. Anyway, he doesn't really believe I'll save enough. But I'm nearly there. I want to see South Africa for myself. I want to make up my own mind.

ROSE: I'm surprised at your father making you work. What a dreadful thing.

ZADOK: Does your Granny know you're coming to see her?

JEREMY: I don't think so.

ROSE: Oh, what a time we'll give you, what a time you'll have, I can't wait to tell Belle —

[*She turns to the window.*]

[*yelling*] Belle, Jeremy's coming to South Africa —

ZADOK: She missed her vocation, she should have been a town
            crier.

[ROSE *sees* BELLE *apparently crying.*]

ROSE: What's happened in there? [*yelling*] Is Belle all right? [*to*
            ZADOK *and* JEREMY] She looks in a terrible state. [*yelling*]
            What's the matter with Belle —?

[LEONARD *switches the switch.*]

            — is she upset, what's the matter with Belle?

[LEONARD *and* BELLE *wince.*]

BELLE: God, I'll go deaf too if you shout like that. [*wiping her eyes*]
            Nothing's the matter. I'm laughing. We had a good
            laugh. Like the old days. Now, I'm dry as a bone. I'd love
            a coffee but I'll settle for water.

ROSE: I'd like coffee, too.

ZADOK: Don't leave me out whatever you do.

LEONARD: Jeremy, there's coffee down the passage. It's only a
            machine, I'm afraid.

ZADOK: These days, everything's a machine —

LEONARD: I'd like one, too. Black for me. Mom?

BELLE: I'll have white.

ROSE: I want a black one, Jeremy.

JEREMY: Uncle Zadok?

ZADOK: Black.

JEREMY: And a black for me. That's four blacks, one white.

[*He goes.*]

ZADOK: Four blacks, one white. It's like being back home.

[*He laughs.*]

ROSE: Has he told you, Belle?

BELLE: Yes, Rose, he's told me.

ROSE: And?

[*Lights fade to blackout.*]

SCENE TWO

*The control booth. Approximately the same time as the previous
scene.*

Through the window LEONARD *can be seen leading* BELLE *out of the
studio. After a moment they appear in the control room, watched*

by ROSE, ZADOK *and* JEREMY, *who are now the ones to be seen but not heard.*

LEONARD: Sit down, Mom, no one can hear us in here.

BELLE: Leonard, before we talk, I have to say something important to you.

LEONARD: What?

BELLE: Your hair's too long.

LEONARD: Mom, I'm fifty-one years old, I've been married and divorced, I'm a father of a grown-up boy, and this is the way I wear my hair.

BELLE: I can't help it, it's still too long. So, what do you have to tell me?

LEONARD: All in good time, it's nothing important.

BELLE: You're not ill, are you?

LEONARD: I'm not ill. Just let's have a nice chat. I've hardly seen you.

BELLE: You haven't changed, Leonard. You were always a bad liar.
[*She notices* ROSE *and the others staring at them.*]
What's she looking at? She's such a nosy woman. I want to tell her something —
[LEONARD *switches the switch.*]

LEONARD: Mom wants to say something.

ROSE: Oh my God, here it comes —

LEONARD: Speak, Mom, they can hear now —

BELLE: I've got this to say. Stop staring at us. You're making me feel as though I'm in a goldfish bowl. [*to* LEONARD] They won't take any notice, Rose probably didn't even hear me, in five minutes she'll be looking again, nosy —
[LEONARD *switches the switch.*]
— you've never known such a nosy woman.

LEONARD: And how's the new flat, Mom?

BELLE: It's small but I bless you every second for it. And the air-conditioner, you don't know the difference that's made. You'll see it when you come back next year. I can't wait.

LEONARD: So, you're sleeping better now?

BELLE: What are you talking about, please, Leonard, who sleeps?
[*An awkward pause.*]

LEONARD: Well, Mom.

BELLE: Sweetheart.

LEONARD: What a long road we've travelled, you and I.

BELLE: Leonard, Leonard.

LEONARD: You look so well.

BELLE: Age is a terrible thing.

LEONARD: You've always looked just the same.

BELLE: From your mouth into God's ear. People say I could pass for seventy-five.

LEONARD: Easily.

BELLE: Yes, yes, you were always such a bad liar. You're sure you're not ill, Leonard?

LEONARD: Mom, I'm not ill.

BELLE: Don't mention your breakdown to Rose and Zadok. It would upset them dreadfully.

LEONARD: You never told them?

BELLE: Are you crazy? They'd have had breakdowns, never mind you. You still have your check-ups?

LEONARD: Mom, I had a C.A.T. scan the other day, I'm absolutely fine.

BELLE: Why didn't you write and tell me?

LEONARD: I've been busy, touring, recording, concerts. You should have told Aunty Rose and Uncle Zadok.

BELLE: Leonard, don't interfere, I know what I'm doing. They've aged terribly. They would never have recovered from the shock. You can see for yourself. With Zadok, I don't know if he's really ga-ga or whether he puts it on. He laughs at his own jokes, always the same jokes, always such old jokes. And Rose. I beg her to get a hearing-aid, but, you know what? She's too vain. What's she got to be vain for? Beats me. Still, they're good for my morale. When I look at them I feel like a young gazelle.

LEONARD: You're sure, when you go back to Cape Town, you don't want to move into a hotel?

BELLE: You mean a home? Don't say hotel when you mean a home, Leonard. I'd die, all those old people, they'd drive me mad. No, I'm better off on my own, independent. Len, tell me honestly, the money you give me every month, can you really afford it? I feel so guilty —

LEONARD: Mom, I can afford it —

BELLE: I don't want to be a burden.

LEONARD: You're not a burden. Do you know what I earn for one concert now? Three, four thousand pounds.

BELLE: For one concert?

LEONARD: Yes, and I give about a hundred concerts a year. Work it
          out for yourself. And then there are my recordings.
          That's another three, four hundred thousand pounds a
          year.
              [*Pause.*]
BELLE: You earn more in one night than I earned in my lifetime.
          Well, well, well. I never thought I'd be able to give up
          work. Here I am, eighty-four, a lady of leisure. I play
          cards with my cronies, all the old girls, mind you, they
          bore me stiff, I'm so easily bored. Sometimes I feel like
          going out to work again.
LEONARD: And you eat properly, Mom, you look after yourself?
BELLE: Leonard, who eats?
              [*Brief silence.* BELLE *is about to speak* —]
LEONARD: Did you get the video I sent? Of the recital in Moscow?
BELLE: Certainly. I think everyone in Cape Town's seen it.
          They're already queueing up to buy tickets for your
          concert next year. And Zadok showed it to the Old Aged
          Home. They've got a video. Seven times he's seen it.
LEONARD: And you?
BELLE: Eight times.
LEONARD: You enjoyed it?
BELLE: Of course.
LEONARD: The Russians were very keen on my Rachmaninoff and
          that was a big compliment, I can tell you.
BELLE: If I may say so, of course I know nothing, but I have
          one criticism. I think you show off too much when you
          play.
LEONARD: What do you mean?
BELLE: People should come and listen to the music, not watch
          the pianist. You sway and you pull faces and you sweat.
          They watch you and they forget the music. It pleases the
          unmusical. A pianist who comes between the audience
          and the music is no pianist. I love music. I don't love
          self-assertion. That's my opinion. I know nothing, but
          it's my opinion. So, next year, when you play in Cape
          Town, a little restraint won't come amiss. Where will
          you stay? The Mount Nelson's a lovely hotel. Fancy,
          Leonard Lands from Sea Point in the Mount Nelson
          Hotel.
              [*Silence.*]
          You're not coming to Cape Town, are you?
              [LEONARD *rises and turns his back on her. In the studio the
              others look into the booth.*]

That's what you had to tell me, isn't it? I can read you like a book, Leonard. I've always read you like a book.

[*In the studio,* JEREMY *helps* ZADOK *to stand.* ZADOK *stamps his feet. Commotion.*]

LEONARD: I'm sorry, Mom, truly I am. It wasn't an easy decision.

BELLE: Politics?

[LEONARD *looks away.*]

Politics, politics, politics.

LEONARD: People, Mom, really, people, people, people —

[ROSE *comes rushing to the window and yells but, of course, they cannot hear her and do not yet see her.*]

BELLE: I hate politics —

LEONARD: [*noticing the fuss in the studio*] What's wrong with Zadok?

BELLE: Oh my God, he's had a heart attack —

[LEONARD *switches a switch.*]

LEONARD: What's the matter?

ROSE: [*yelling*] Zadok's got cramp!

BELLE: I thought he was having a heart attack.

ZADOK: It's gone. It's all right. Don't make a fuss. I'm fine.

ROSE: [*to the booth, yelling*] He's fine.

BELLE: I can hear, thank you.

ROSE: He's as fit as a fiddle.

ZADOK: From your mouth into God's ear.

ROSE: [*whispering*] Everything all right, Belle?

BELLE: [*to* LEONARD] She doesn't realise the microphone's on.

[LEONARD *switches the switch.*]

[*to* ROSE, *who can't hear*] Rose, the microphone's on, they can hear you all over the building, they can probably hear you in Piccadilly Circus —

[ROSE *yells at the window.*]

Is it on or off, Leonard? For God's sake, I'll have a nervous breakdown, stop playing with —

[LEONARD *switches the switch again.*]

— the switch.

LEONARD: It's on.

BELLE: You're sure?

LEONARD: Yes, I'm sure.

BELLE: All right, then. [*to the studio*] Please leave us in peace, my son and I are having a private conversation.

[LEONARD *switches the switch. Silence in the booth.*]

Well. So. There we are. You're not going to give a recital in your own home town.

LEONARD: No.

BELLE: Why not?

LEONARD: Because.

BELLE: Leonard, 'because' isn't good enough.

LEONARD: Because everyone has to make their protest in their own way. I have only my music. It's a gesture, that's all, pathetic, ineffectual, but a gesture. And it has to be made.

BELLE: All these years I waited for this one thing. You, giving a recital, being acclaimed in your own home town.

LEONARD: Mom, I have to make a stand.

BELLE: You have to make a stand. Against your own mother?

LEONARD: Oh, Mom, don't be ridiculous —

BELLE: Ridiculous? Ridiculous? Is it ridiculous to ask for a little pleasure out of life? Think of the pleasure you'd give me. Is it such a terrible thing to ask for a little pleasure? When spirits are low, when I'm bored, I think of you, marching on to the stage in Cape Town, the audience rising to greet you, you bowing, and me, sitting there, like a queen, glowing, bursting with pride and pleasure. Is that such a terrible thing to ask?

LEONARD: Mom, believe me, I don't mean to hurt you.

BELLE: Thanks very much, God help me when you do mean it. All right. You won't play in South Africa. That's your decision. That's your right. We won't discuss it again.

LEONARD: Thank you.

BELLE: But why did you tell Rose you weren't coming before you told me?

LEONARD: It just came out.

BELLE: It just came out. Good, that's another reason I'm not speaking to you.

LEONARD: What d'you mean, another reason?

BELLE: That interview you gave.

LEONARD: What interview?

BELLE: In the magazine, with the picture of you in Tokyo —

LEONARD: Mom, I've given a few interviews in my time —

BELLE: Never mind, you know the one I mean —

LEONARD: I don't know what you're talking about.

BELLE: Don't get short with me, Leonard.

LEONARD: What interview?

BELLE: Where you said you came from an unhappy marriage.

LEONARD: Well, I did.

BELLE: I know your father was a very difficult man, but why tell the world?

LEONARD: You want me to lie?

BELLE: Leonard, don't be so clever, your fame doesn't impress me. How can you say such things in public?

LEONARD: Mom, the man asked me —

BELLE: You said being the product of an unhappy marriage had affected you deeply.

LEONARD: That's true —

BELLE: How can you say such a thing, Leonard? Can you imagine my embarrassment?

LEONARD: Mom, everyone knows you and Dad weren't happy.

BELLE: But in print, Leonard, in print. No, I think it was very wrong of you —

LEONARD: Mom, it was the making of me —

BELLE: What was?

LEONARD: You and Dad, the unhappiness —

BELLE: Leonard, please, I don't want to talk about it —

LEONARD: Without that pain —

BELLE: What pain? What are you talking about? What pain? You were never in pain. You exaggerate, you strike attitudes, you had a wonderful childhood, everything your heart desired I gave you. What pain, what pain, what do you know about pain?

LEONARD: Mom, pain was the making of me.
    [*Silence.*]

BELLE: Well, that's all right, then.
    [*Silence.*]
That's why I worry about Jeremy.

LEONARD: What's Jeremy got to do with it?

BELLE: I'm worried about him, that's what he's got to do with it.

LEONARD: Jeremy's all right —

BELLE: I didn't say he wasn't. He's a beautiful boy, I could eat him up, the way he speaks, oh God, what a boy, but I'm worried about him.

LEONARD: Why, for God's sake?

BELLE: Because he's very unhappy. I can tell. He doesn't say much.

LEONARD: Mom, people who don't say much aren't necessarily unhappy.

BELLE: He's withdrawn, he's remote. And he drives that car as if he's trying to kill himself and all his passengers. Thank God Zadok's ga-ga, he would have had a heart attack if he'd noticed the way that boy drives.

LEONARD: Mom, the way Jeremy drives doesn't make him unhappy.

BELLE: I only had to mention your name, he accelerates to a hundred miles an hour and drives at the first car he sees. You think I don't notice these things?

> [*Pause.*]

Has he got girl friends?

LEONARD: I don't know, yes, I think so, I don't know —

BELLE: You want to be careful with him, you know what I mean.

LEONARD: I don't know what you mean —

> [BELLE *moistens her third finger and then smoothes her eyebrow.* LEONARD *laughs.*]

Don't be ridiculous, he's perfectly normal.

BELLE: I always used to say to Rose, if I hear Lennie's turned into a 'nice' boy — [*the gesture again*] — I'll take a pair of scissors, I'll go to England and I'll cut it off.

> [LEONARD *laughs quietly.*]

You must face it, Leonard. Your son is miserable. And you know why?

> [*No response.*]

Because you should never have divorced Stella.

LEONARD: Mom, I don't want to discuss this —

BELLE: You should have crawled to her on your hands and knees and begged her to come back —

LEONARD: Mom —

BELLE: For Jeremy's sake you should have done that.

LEONARD: It was better for Jeremy we got divorced.

BELLE: Don't say such things to me. You think I endured twenty-five years of hell with your father to be told we should have got divorced? Your father and I didn't get divorced, because of you, for your happiness, for your well-being, for your future —

LEONARD: Mom, please, don't talk such nonsense —

BELLE: Leonard, don't speak to me like that —

LEONARD: I don't want to talk about Stella —

BELLE: You don't want to talk about Stella —

LEONARD: No, I don't want to talk about her —

BELLE: You think I enjoyed the rows —

LEONARD: I don't know —

BELLE: You don't know —

LEONARD: No, I don't know —

BELLE: You think I enjoyed the misery —

LEONARD: Mom, I don't care any more —

BELLE: You don't care —

LEONARD: I don't care any more, I don't care, I don't care, I don't care —

BELLE: That's your trouble, Leonard, you've never cared.

LEONARD: Good, fine, terrific, I never cared —

BELLE: You've never cared about another living soul. Only yourself —

LEONARD: That's right, only myself, that's all I've cared about, only myself —

BELLE: Me, me, me, me. You think I don't understand these things?

LEONARD: No, no, I know you understand everything —

BELLE: I understand very well. I don't want you to send me another penny —

LEONARD: What are you talking about now?

BELLE: It's exactly the same as you play the piano. You pose. You strike attitudes. But feeling for people, caring, for your own flesh and blood, never. You give me my allowance and you don't have to think about me for another month. You let Stella walk out on you, and you send Jeremy to boarding-school and he can go to hell for all you care. And when it comes to giving your mother a little pleasure and playing in your own home town, which gave you life, which made you what you are, to play in front of your mother and her family and her friends, what do you do? You strike an attitude. Suddenly you're a political figure —

LEONARD: I'm not talking about you and your pleasure —

BELLE: Don't tell me, I know —

LEONARD: I'm talking about making a stand —

BELLE: You're talking, you're talking, yes, talking —

LEONARD: I didn't ask to be born in South Africa —

BELLE: No, *I* asked for it.

LEONARD: Shut up, Mom, shut up!

> [BELLE *is shocked for a moment, then she weeps.*]

I'm sorry. I'm sorry.

> [ROSE *comes to the window.* BELLE *sees her through her tears.* ROSE *continues to talk.*]

BELLE: What did I tell you? There she is. Give me a moment, I'll pull myself together, switch that switch, Leonard, do as I say for once in your life —

> [LEONARD *reaches out and switches the switch.*]

ROSE: [*her voice booming*] — is she upset, what's the matter with Belle?

> [BELLE *and* LEONARD *wince.*]

BELLE: God, I'll go deaf too if you shout like that. [*wiping her eyes*] Nothing's the matter. I'm laughing. We had a good laugh. Like the old days. Now, I'm dry as a bone. I'd love a coffee but I'll settle for water.

ROSE: I'd like coffee, too.

ZADOK: Don't leave me out whatever you do.

LEONARD: [*forcing a smile*] Jeremy, there's coffee down the passage. It's only a machine, I'm afraid.

ZADOK: These days, everything's a machine —

LEONARD: I'd like one, too. Black for me. Mom?

BELLE: I'll have white.

ROSE: I want a black one, Jeremy.

JEREMY: Uncle Zadok?

ZADOK: Black.

JEREMY: And a black for me. That's four blacks, one white. [*He goes.*]

ZADOK: Four blacks, one white. It's like being back home. [*He laughs.*]

ROSE: Has he told you, Belle?

BELLE: Yes, Rose, he's told me.

ROSE: And?

BELLE: [*sharply*] And. [*Lights fade to blackout.*]

SCENE THREE

The studio, the moment after the last scene ends.

BELLE *enters the studio.*

ROSE: Are you upset, Belle?

BELLE: I'm not easily upset.

ROSE: I've got something to cheer you up.

ZADOK: Jeremy's coming to Cape Town.

ROSE: [*turning on him*] *I* was going to tell her —

ZADOK: So, I beat you to it —

BELLE: Jeremy's coming to Cape Town? When?

ROSE: You've become very vindictive in your old age, Zadok.

ZADOK: As I always say, there's no justice in the world.

BELLE: Where is he, where is he? I want to see that boy —

ROSE: He's working to save the money. Leonard's matching him pound for pound —

BELLE: You should only know how much he earns. He's a millionaire and he talks about nothing but money.

ZADOK: I wonder who he takes after.

BELLE: Modern parents, they make you sick —

[JEREMY *returns with the coffee.*]

Jeremy, when you come to Cape Town you'll stay with me. The room's no bigger than a cupboard but at least it will save you paying for a hotel.

[JEREMY *hands out the coffees.*]

[*continuing*] Someone'll lend you a car, people are very generous. They'll make such a fuss of you, mark my words. You'll meet lots of young people, lots of pretty girls, oh, the girls, Jeremy, you'll love the girls, you'll go to the beach, get a nice tan, what a time you'll have.

JEREMY: Thank you, Gran.

BELLE: [*confidential*] And listen, I've got a little saved from the money your father gives me each month, you're welcome to it.

JEREMY: Gran, it's not necessary —

BELLE: I'll decide what's necessary. I want you to have the money.

[JEREMY *kisses her on the cheek. She glows.*]

ROSE: And do you read many books, Jeremy?

JEREMY: Not too many. I read music. Dad taught me. He's going to let me turn the pages for him today. Isn't that nice?

ROSE: When you come to Cape Town, you've got the run of my library. Over two thousand volumes and no rubbish.

JEREMY: Thank you.

[ZADOK *stands and crosses to* JEREMY.]

ZADOK: And, Jeremy, will you come and see me in the Old Aged Home?

JEREMY: Of course.

ZADOK: I'll make them put something special on the menu for you. Instead of rice pudding with jam, they'll give you jam with rice pudding.

JEREMY: I like rice pudding.

ZADOK: Hold my sticks.

[JEREMY *does so.* ZADOK *squeezes his cheeks with grunts of pleasure.*]

That boy, I could eat him.

[LEONARD *enters the studio.*]

LEONARD: Perhaps I owe you all an explanation.

BELLE: Leonard, you owe us nothing. There's nothing to explain. What time do you start recording?

ROSE: You know, Leonard, I was thinking, if next year you did come back and play in South Africa, it would have been longer than in *The Winter's Tale*.

ZADOK: What are you talking about now, Rose?

ROSE: The time gap. 'Impute it not a crime/To me or my swift passage, that I slide/O'er sixteen years, and leave the growth/untried of that wide gap.' In Shakespeare it's sixteen years before we get back to Bohemia. With Leonard it would have been thirty-six before he played the piano again in Cape Town.

ZADOK: So, with Shakespeare you get it wholesale.
    [*He loves this.*]

ROSE: Ignore him, Jeremy. It's premature senility.

ZADOK: What d'you mean, premature? I'm eighty-nine, I'm bang on schedule.

BELLE: [*to* LEONARD] What time do you start to record?

LEONARD: The technicians should be back in about twenty minutes.

ZADOK: British workmen.

ROSE: [*to* ZADOK, *a whisper*] Belle's upset, I can see she's upset —

BELLE: Who's upset?

ROSE: Belle, I know you must be upset.

BELLE: About what?

ROSE: About what, she says. About Leonard, of course, about him not coming out. You must be upset.

BELLE: I'm not so easily upset, Rose. And I've got Jeremy to look forward to.

ROSE: Never mind Jeremy, you've talked about nothing else for years. Leonard, at the piano, in Cape Town.

BELLE: What will be, will be.

ROSE: You see? You're upset.

BELLE: Rose, I'm not upset.

ROSE: Not much.

BELLE: Rose, I'll scream in a moment.

ROSE: Scream, it'll do you good.

BELLE: You scream, leave me out of it.
    [*Long pause.*]
    God, I hate politics!

ROSE: You see, I told you she's upset.

ZADOK: In the old days, Jeremy, when your father was a boy, we never talked politics. It was strictly *verboten*.

LEONARD: The world's changed, Uncle Zadok.

ZADOK: Don't I know? I'll tell you how much the world's changed, and I've seen it all. In the thirties, for example, no one stopped buying cameras from the Germans. No one stopped inviting Ribbentrop to

Cliveden, no one boycotted the Berlin Olympics, that's how much the world's changed. Now the world is full of saints and Mahatma Gandhis.

LEONARD: And about time.

ZADOK: You see, Jeremy, I'm a Pavlovian, a disciple of the Russian psychologist, Pavlov.

ROSE: So, where's your dog?

ZADOK: A very well-read woman, your great-aunt Rose. Listen and learn, Rose, it's never too late. Yes, Pavlov. I believe in the conditioned reflex. I believe everybody in this world is conditioned by where they were born, grew up and lived their formative years. This is not a profound thought. In fact, it's a commonplace. But, there are conclusions to be drawn nevertheless. And the conclusion is, we all think we would behave better in somebody else's country. We all know better when it comes to somebody else. But ourselves? Each man bestows upon his own native heath sanctity. Remember that, because that's my last word on the subject.

BELLE: Good, fine, now let's talk about something else. Promise me we won't mention politics again.

ZADOK: I promise. We'll talk about something else. Did I tell you, Jeremy, we've got a video machine in the Old Aged Home?

JEREMY: No —

ZADOK: Yes. We've got a video machine and they show us films, two, three times a week. One Sunday afternoon they showed *The Godfather*. What a film. Maybe the second-best film I've ever seen. It's about a fellow born in Sicily who goes to America and becomes the head of the Mafia, *capo di capi*, the godfather of all godfathers. And what he does to people and what people do to him, you wouldn't believe. But the film is a film with a moral. Ask me what the moral is.

JEREMY: What's the moral, Uncle Zadok?

ZADOK: The moral of the film is, don't get born in Sicily.
         [*He loves this.*]

ROSE: This man is totally insane.

BELLE: God, you're devious, Zadok.

ZADOK: Jeremy, you want to know the best film I've ever seen?

BELLE: No, he doesn't —

ZADOK: Yes, he does. It's a newsreel, Jeremy, Ask me, what newsreel?

JEREMY: What newsreel, Uncle Zadok?

ZADOK: The one where Jesse Owens wins a gold medal at the
        Berlin Olympics in 1936. He beats the whole Master
        Race, and Hitler leaves the stadium as though he's just
        been told he's got prostate trouble. I love that film.

JEREMY: Dad's only cancelled his concert because he wants to
        impress Mummy.

LEONARD: Jeremy, shut up —

JEREMY: That was one of the very big rows between them —

LEONARD: Jeremy, I'm going to slap you hard —

JEREMY: Mummy said you had double standards, Dad. You see,
        he's played in Turkey, in Czechoslovakia, in Russia.
        Where's he going to stop? Will he play the piano in
        Ethiopia? In Malawi? Libya? Iran?

ROSE: What are you, Jeremy, a gazeteer?

JEREMY: I simply want to know where one draws the line.

        [LEONARD *slaps* JEREMY *across the face.* JEREMY *runs out
        and re-appears in the control booth.*]
        [*Silence.*]

ROSE: And we wanted to come back to London before we died.

ZADOK: Afterwards wouldn't be such fun.
        [*Silence.*]
        [LEONARD *marches up to the control booth window.*]

LEONARD: [*mouthing, a tense whisper*] Come — back — in — here!
        [JEREMY *ignores him.*]

BELLE: Leonard, leave him, please, he'll come back. Control
        yourself. Where's your self-control? And I beg you, no
        more, I don't want this aggravation —
        [*She controls her tears.*]

LEONARD: I won't have Jeremy speak to me like that.

BELLE: [*to* ROSE] You see what a broken marriage does to a
        child?

ROSE: I told you she was upset

BELLE: Rose, you want me to be upset, I'll be upset, I'm going
        to kill you in a moment and then I won't be upset.
        [*Silence.*]

LEONARD: Let me just say this —

BELLE: We don't want to hear, we understand what you do is
        your own business, we don't want to hear —

LEONARD: Look, whatever I am, whatever I've become, the price
        was paid not by me, not by Mom or Dad, or by any of us
        here, but by a great mass of people who had no say in the
        matter. I was able to flourish at their expense. And for
        that I feel ashamed, deeply, deeply ashamed. I can't
        help it, that's what I feel.

ZADOK: But where's your pity?

LEONARD: What d'you mean, where's my pity?

ZADOK: What about us? Where's your pity for us? You should feel pity for the oppressors and the oppressed. There are two sides to every story.

           [*Silence.*]

           You know your trouble, Leonard? You've never been very bright. And I'll tell you something else. After a lifetime of serious study, in my opinion nothing can be explained.

BELLE: Then why do you explain everything?

LEONARD: [*angered*] Listen to me, for God's sake, listen to me! The trouble is, you won't listen, you don't want to hear!

BELLE: Leonard, I've decided. I don't want you to come to my funeral.

ZADOK: What's she say?

ROSE: She doesn't want Leonard to come to her funeral.

ZADOK: What's she talking about, she's not dead yet, is she?

ROSE: God forbid, Zadok, that's a terrible thing to say.

ZADOK: She doesn't look dead to me —

BELLE: My mind's made up. Don't waste money on a fruitless journey. I'd rather Jeremy had the money.

LEONARD: Mom, cancelling my concert in Cape Town is my only weapon —

BELLE: I'm not talking about your concert, I'm talking about my funeral.

ROSE: Wait a moment, wait a moment, before we bury you, Belle, I want to ask your son something.

BELLE: I don't want to be buried, I want to be cremated. I've left it in my will.

ROSE: Wait a moment. You said weapon, Leonard, what weapon are you talking about? You're not a soldier, for God's sake, you're a musician, an artist —

LEONARD: Aunty Rose, being an artist is not some divine job description —

ROSE: Not divine? Being an artist is not divine? What a terrible thing to say —

ZADOK: And by the way, there are two things that have never brought a government to its knees. Sanctions and bombing the civilian population.

LEONARD: Oh, really, Uncle Zadok? What about Hiroshima?

ZADOK: Hey, that's not bad, Len, I'll try to remember that —

ROSE: Believe it or not, I, too, have something to say. It's no secret I'm a lover of books, a lover of poetry, a lover of art. I believe in art, that's what I believe in. God I leave to the godly, business and politics I leave to crooks. I believe in art. I believe art — I mean literature, poetry, the theatre, music, painting, ballet, the opera — all art is an expression of what's best about each and every one of us. All right, so I'm a deaf, old spinster who knows nothing, who's never been in love, who's never been loved —

BELLE: Never been loved? How can you say you've never been loved, Rose? That's a terrible thing to say —

ROSE: All right, all right, let me finish. I know people laugh at me behind my back, I know what people say about me, I know, I know, I know. But no one will take my belief away from me, and my belief is that art is a solace, art is a benediction. All right, argue with me, shout me down, call me an old fool who knows nothing of life, but my world was created, transformed and blessed by art. My prayers are for more Shakespeares and George Eliots, my litany is to the glory of Mozart and Schubert, my worship is of Rembrandt and Chagall, and the infinite number of artists whose vision has made me able to bear this life from one day to the next. Where would we have been, Belle, you and I, without our poetry, without our Browning, our Wordsworth, our Byron? There's not a thought in my head, not a feeling in my body that art hasn't, in one way or another, informed and fired. And this is what I have against you, Leonard, whom I love with all my heart, this: that you withhold from your great mass of people whom you claim paid for your privileges, you deny them as well as us, your ability to bring forth musical sounds which adds to the glory of being alive. Leonard, are you listening to me? You want to feel ashamed? Feel ashamed you've cancelled your concert. You must hold your talent in very low esteem because it seems you believe deep down that not one note you play will change a single human heart. That's where I disagree with you. You see, stupid old woman that I am, I believe there's a chance that music might, might, just might, turn the whole world upside down, all right, not the whole world, I don't believe in miracles, but one individual world, and that's a chance, in my opinion,

you're meant to take. After all, I speak from personal
experience. That's it, that's what I believe, I'm finished,
now make fun of me.
[*Silence.*]

ZADOK: Sister mine, you make me weep, me, a dry, dusty —

BELLE: All right, Zadok, we know, we know.
[*Silence.*]

LEONARD: You're talking about another time, Aunty Rose,
Those things belong to another time.

BELLE: More's the pity. Everything seems like a thousand years
ago to me. I don't think about the past. I had such hopes
— I hate the past.

ROSE: Anyway, you've got Jeremy to look forward to.

ZADOK: Kitchener died and England won the war.

BELLE: His mind's wandering, ignore him.

ROSE: You won't think again, Len?
[*Silence.*]

ZADOK: Where's Jeremy?
[ZADOK *rises. He goes to the control booth window and makes
signs to catch* JEREMY's *attention.* JEREMY *switches the
switch.*]
Are you receiving me loud and clear?

JEREMY: Yes.

ZADOK: Come back here, I've got something to ask you.

JEREMY: I can hear you, Uncle Zadok.

ZADOK: Fine, it's a difficult question. What do you think of your
father's peculiar family?

JEREMY: At least you talk about what matters to each other —

ZADOK: Wrong. We skirt the issues, same as everyone else,
only we do it more loudly.
[*He laughs.*]

JEREMY: It makes me feel I'm alive.

ZADOK: From your mouth into God's ear. You have only one
obligation, and that's to life. That's what's kept us all so
young. You know what they call me, Jeremy, in Cape
Town? Peter Pan. The boy who never grew up.

BELLE: Jeremy, darling, come back in here, please, for my
sake —
[JEREMY *switches the switch and leaves the control booth.*]
You should apologise to him, Leonard. What you did
was uncalled for —

LEONARD: He should apologise to me. And, Mom, don't interfere.
[JEREMY *re-enters the studio.*]

BELLE: Come and sit by me, Jeremy.

[*He does so.*]

Fathers, eh, Jeremy?

ZADOK: And mothers.

LEONARD: I'll tell you something, Mom, I think often of Dad, of my father —

BELLE: You can do what you like, it's not my business.

ZADOK: I was very fond of Ike. He had the biggest store of useless information of any man I've ever met. Yet he never knew who he was, what he was, and he had no chance in life, but I liked him. And his father was a wonderful whistler. That's where Leonard gets his talent from.

BELLE: For a clever man, Zadok, you talk more rubbish than anyone else. There was no talent in that family at all. Ike's father. Please. He could hardly read or write let alone whistle.

LEONARD: I wish I'd talked to Dad more —

ROSE: You see, I told you, they never talked.

BELLE: How could anyone talk to Ike? He had nothing to say except the world was against him —

LEONARD: Nevertheless, listen to me. This is interesting —

ZADOK: We'll be the judge of that.

LEONARD: I think now it was as if he and I were, somehow, conspirators.

ROSE: What?

LEONARD: Conspirators!

ROSE: Who?

LEONARD: Me and Dad.

ROSE: You and Ike?

ZADOK: I told you there was something between them.

BELLE: Between whom? Between Ike and Leonard? Please, you're talking about chalk and cheese. And, Leonard, you never cried when he died. I'll never forget that, it upset me for weeks —

ZADOK: I told you, he was always a bottled-up boy.

LEONARD: We were conspirators. We shared a secret. You know what we shared? A sense of failure.

BELLE: Leonard, I've never heard anything so ridiculous in all my life. You a failure? What's success, then? I don't believe I'm hearing these words.

LEONARD: He felt he was washed up in the wrong place at the wrong time.

BELLE: I never heard him say anything like that.

LEONARD: You never talked to him, so how could you hear?

BELLE: Leonard, please, not in front of Jeremy, please —

LEONARD: Well, I remember. And it comes back to me, and it haunts me. When I was a kid, in Cape Town, I used to go down to the beach and spit in the sea.

ROSE: He used to do what?

ZADOK: Spit in the sea. Like old Abe Bendel. He spits, in the sea, on the carpet, in his bed, you've never seen such a spitter.

[ROSE *and* BELLE *laugh.*]

LEONARD: All right, you don't want to hear, I won't tell you —

ROSE: We want to hear —

LEONARD: Just so that I can get this off my chest, I'll tell you as quickly as I can. Because I want you to know. I used to spit in the sea and watch my saliva disintegrate into millions of undetectable particles, still me, but also part of the ocean being carried who knows where, reaching out to other islands, seas, continents, other people, all people, eternity, the whole universe. I was at one with the world. I felt I embraced the world.

ZADOK: All this from spitting in the sea?

LEONARD: All right, all right, very funny, but the point is this. I've never felt that again. Even here, where I've lived most of my life, I'm not at home.

BELLE: You've lived in this country thirty-five years and you don't feel at home here?

ROSE: How can you say you're not at home in London? It's not possible.

ZADOK: Perhaps he should spit in the sea more often.

LEONARD: The truth is, I'm an alien wherever I am.

ROSE: I don't understand this. What more does he want? What more is there? You play your music all over the world —

JEREMY: Except in South Africa —

LEONARD: Jeremy, when I need another comment from you I'll ask for it.

BELLE: Jeremy, darling, enough now.

LEONARD: Aunty Rose, I wanted, I wanted — what did I want? I think all I wanted was to be somebody.

ROSE: So?

LEONARD: [*smiling*] I still want to be somebody. That's why — I don't know — perhaps that's why I do what I do. Perhaps that's why I'm making this stand. Stella said I had no backbone. Perhaps this is my backbone.

BELLE: Why you're not coming to Cape Town to play? To be somebody? To have a backbone?

LEONARD: Perhaps. I don't know. I tell you these things because I don't want you to think that the decision was easily arrived at.

ZADOK: I'll tell you something, Leonard. It's not where you are, it's who you are.

LEONARD: Who am I, that's the point, who am I?

ZADOK: 'The fault, dear Brutus, lies not in our stars but in ourselves —'

LEONARD: Yes, yes, yes, yes —

BELLE: Zadok, no more philosophy, please, it drives me mad —

ZADOK: Fine. Not another aphorism do I utter. Except this. There's no justice in this world.

LEONARD: As my father used to say.

ZADOK: I said it —

LEONARD: No, Uncle Zadok, my Dad said it —

BELLE: Leonard, forgive me, now you're talking nonsense. How could your father say such a thing? Leonard's father, Jeremy, your grandfather, was a very simple man. Difficult, but very simple. Mind you, he never raised a finger to Leonard. But all he knew was what a bad hand he was dealt.

LEONARD: All right, all right, whoever said it.

ZADOK: I said it.

LEONARD: All right, all right! You've all believed in me so much for so long, perhaps it's now time I should believe in myself.

JEREMY: Cue music.

LEONARD: Shut up, Jeremy.

JEREMY: No, I won't shut up, because I can't talk to you when we're alone. You take the easy way out, that's what I can't stand, you take the easy way out —

BELLE: Jeremy —

JEREMY: Not going to South Africa is easier, because if you wanted to make a real stand, you'd go. But no, no, you do what's expected of you because it's easier. And all the talk about the great suffering masses. I always like that bit, Dad, when you become so impassioned about the great suffering masses while you sip your champagne in the back of a chauffeur-driven car doing the social whirl —

ZADOK: Now, that's unfair, Jeremy. You mustn't blame your father for enjoying what the world pays him. And you don't have to be good to do good, remember that —

BELLE: Zadok, don't interfere —

JEREMY: And the music he plays, he plays what comes easiest to him. Rachmaninoff. All the critics say he plays too much Rachmaninoff —

BELLE: I read those critics, Jeremy. They were Germans. Enough said.

LEONARD: Jeremy, please don't talk of things you know absolutely nothing about. When I first played the piano —

ROSE: In my flat, above the library, a Mozart minuet, I remember it as if it were yesterday, he was five years old —

LEONARD: Yes, I was five years old. I just went to the piano and played. Gran didn't arrange for me to have lessons in the hope that I'd have talent. The talent came first, and she arranged for lessons as a result. Talent has always been the taskmaster, and, yes, I don't deny, in certain respects, it came easily to me. At nine years old I sight-read the Beethoven C minor piano concerto. But it wasn't just a sight-reading, it was a *performance*, as though I'd worked on the piece for months. And everyone marvelled, and I couldn't understand why because it was as natural to me as drawing breath. And it still comes naturally to me, yet why is it I have to practise and that some times I play sublimely and others like a blacksmith? On the good days I don't suddenly develop extra fingers or muscles, I don't have bionic arms or a computerised nervous system. So why is it that some times I have to struggle and fight and, yes, Mom, hammer the keys until the sweat pours down my face and back? Why? What's the problem, what's the secret? The problem is that the world impinges. When you're nine years old, or on the good days, you and the world are one, or there is no world, or there's just your world. The truth is, I can only play really well when the chasm between who I am and what I do disappears. That's why I practise. I practise to make the piece I play easy so that my physical actions are secondary to everything else. That's how it is. What I am is how I play. Yes, and I enjoy cigars and champagne and parties and restaurants because I need to be with people, and because most of my life I spend alone at a piano, or in foreign hotel rooms, after a concert, watching television programmes in languages I don't understand. And I play Rachmaninoff, Jeremy, because his soulfulness puts me directly in touch with my own emotions, aspirations, doubts, insecurities, innermost feelings.

And I require that, like a drug. Because what I am is how I play.

BELLE: Is that what you meant when you said pain was the making of you?

[*Silence.*]

I must have done something wrong. I don't want to think about it, I can't bear to think about these things, and I was so looking forward to — [*breaks off*] Everything's poisoned. Where's the pleasure in life? Where's the pleasure?

LEONARD: [*to* BELLE] Dad used to talk about being in the wrong place at the wrong time. I feel that. I curse the fact I was born where I was born. It's crippled me.

BELLE: Leonard, you're driving daggers through my heart —

LEONARD: And I am obsessed by the impermanence of things and I remember Dad talking about being swept away — he used to talk to you, Uncle Zadok, about these things — about sudden disaster, volcanic eruptions, you remember, Uncle Zadok?

ZADOK: I never heard Ike mention a volcanic eruption in his life. He had trouble with his bowels, that I remember —

[ROSE *and* BELLE *laugh and so does* JEREMY, *and, eventually,* LEONARD, *too.* ZADOK *chuckles and wheezes. They all become a little hysterical.* LEONARD'*s laughter turns to tears. He sobs. The others stop laughing.* LEONARD *holds out a hand.* BELLE *hesitates, then takes it.* LEONARD *cries.*]

[TWO TECHNICIANS *enter the control room. One of them switches the switch.*]

TECHNICIAN: We're back, Maestro. Ready to record?

[*All, except* LEONARD, *swing round to look at the booth.* LEONARD *continues to cry.*]

[*Lights fade to blackout.*]

SCENE FOUR

The control room, an hour later.

In the studio LEONARD *records a Rachmaninoff prelude: 'Elégie, Opus 3, No. 1. He plays with great stillness.* JEREMY *turns the pages for him.*

The music is relayed into the control room where BELLE *sits between* ROSE *and* ZADOK, *behind the* TWO TECHNICIANS, *who wear headphones.*

ZADOK *sleeps.* ROSE *listens with a sweet, unwavering smile. It is uncertain whether or not she hears what is being said.*

BELLE: He never looked like Ronald Colman.
[*They listen.*]
No, no, no, Rose, I'm not going to think about the past.
[*She takes out a handkerchief and wipes her eyes, blows her nose.*]
You see, he's been my life for so long. Sometimes I ask myself why we have children.
[*They listen.*]
No, no, all's right with the world.
[*They listen.*]
Videos, broadcasts, recordings, that's all I ever hear of him these days. Where's the life, Rose, where's the life?
[*They listen.*]
Rose, in confidence, I gave him such a piece of my mind when we were alone. Did I let him have it. Mind you, I think he's playing better as a result. He's not pulling faces, he's not swaying, he's not sweating, altogether less self.
[*They listen.*]
My honest opinion is that Jeremy won't come to Cape Town either. Is Leonard going to have trouble with that boy? Well, what can you expect from a broken home? Oh, Rose, children, children.
[*They listen.*]
Never mind children, this child, this particular child, this Leonard of mine, light of my life. He's been a perpetual excitement to me. I remember him setting off, carrying all my dreams and hopes and longings. What a blessing promise is. I still pray every night. But never for myself, never. You should pray, Rose, although if God heard from you after all these years he'd probably die of shock.
[*They listen.*]
You know what Miss Katz said to me the last time I saw her alive? She said she envied me. I told her she needed her head examined. With all that money and she envied me.
[*They listen.*]

I'm going to tell you something in absolute confidence, Rose. I'm pleased he's not coming back to Cape Town. I'm pleased he's cancelled the concert. I'd never tell him to his face but I think he made the right decision. Not because I think he's going to change the world. On the contrary. I don't have to tell you or Zadok what a terrible century this has been. No, I don't think one man's protest will change the world. But I've learned a lesson and for that I thank him. I used to think people couldn't change. Maybe I'm an exception. Rose, you know what I've learned? To let go. He's been my life for too long. We can't cling forever. I think everybody has to learn to let go.

[*They listen.*]

I've never minded anything so long as there's a purpose.

[*They listen.*]

Let's just hope things get better, not worse.

[*They listen.*]

This is odd. I used to have a feeling of terrible foreboding. It's gone now. It was like a premonition, I'd go to sleep with it, I'd wake with it, I just knew that something terrible was going to happen, a catastrophe, a disaster, something awful. But it's gone now. And you know why I think it's gone? Because perhaps it's happened.

[*They listen.*]

Who knows? Who knows?

[*They listen.*]

Where does he get it from? Where, where, where does he get it from?

[*They listen.*]

Leonard, oh my Leonard.

ROSE: Your Leonard, Belle, and Ike's.

BELLE: What she shouldn't hear she hears.

ROSE: And Ike, Belle. Yes, Belle, and Ike.

BELLE: Yes, yes, all right. [*Pause; irritably, sharp*] And Ike.

[LEONARD *finishes the piece triumphantly.*]

[ROSE *rises and applauds wildly.*]

[ZADOK *wakes and struggles to his feet.*]

ZADOK: Bravo! Bravo!

[ROSE *and* ZADOK *applaud.*]

[THE TECHNICIANS *look back at them.*]

[BELLE *glows.*]

[*Lights fade to blackout.*]

Other books by Ronald Harwood

Novels

All the Same Shadows
The Guilt Merchants
The Girl in Melanie Klein
Articles of Faith
The Genoa Ferry
Cesar and Augusta

Short Stories:

One. Interior. Day. *Adventures in the Film Trade*

Biography:

Sir Donald Wolfit CBE: *His life and work in the unfashionable theatre**

Plays:

A Family
The Ordeal of Gilbert Pinfold (from Evelyn Waugh)*
The Dresser*
After the Lions*
Tramway Road*
The Deliberate Death of a Polish Priest*
Interpreters*
J.J. Farr*
Ivanov (Chekhov: English version)*

Miscellaneous:

A Night at the Theatre (Editor)
The Ages of Gielgud (Editor)
All the World's a Stage
Mandela
Dear Alec (Editor)

*Published by Amber Lane Press